Focus on Fitness and Wellness

Department of Health and Exercise Studies
North Carolina State University

Sixth Edition

macmillan learning
curriculum solutions

bedford/st.martin's ▪ hayden-mcneil ▪ w.h. freeman ▪ worth publishers

Printed in the United States of America

10 9 8 7 6 5 4 3 2 1

ISBN 978-0-7380-8584-5

Macmillan Learning Curriculum Solutions
14903 Pilot Drive
Plymouth, MI 48170
www.macmillanlearning.com

Koutroumpis 8584-5 F16

Hayden-McNeil Sustainability

Hayden-McNeil's standard paper stock uses a minimum of 30% post-consumer waste. We offer higher % options by request, including a 100% recycled stock. Additionally, Hayden-McNeil Custom Digital provides authors with the opportunity to convert print products to a digital format. Hayden-McNeil is part of a larger sustainability initiative through Macmillan Learning. Visit http://sustainability.macmillan.com to learn more.

HEALTH AND EXERCISE STUDIES

Health and Exercise Studies Courses

ACTIVITY COURSES		
HESF 100 Cross Training	HESA 231 Scientific Diving	HESO 262 Introduction to Whitewater Canoeing
HESF 101 Fitness and Wellness	HESD 233 Clogging	
HESF 102 Fitness Walking	HESD 234 Country Dance	HESD 263 Tap Dance
HESF 103 Water Aerobics	HESS 235 Karate	HESD 264 Ballet
HESF 104 Swim Conditioning	HESF 237 Weight Training	HEST 265 Softball
HESF 105 Aerobics and Body Conditioning	HESS 239 Self Defense	HEST 266 Ultimate Frisbee
	HESD 240 Social Dance	HEST 267 Flag Football
HESF 106 Triathlon	HESD 241 Social Dance II	HEST 269 Volleyball I
HESF 107 Run Conditioning	HESR 242 Badminton	HEST 270 Volleyball II
HESF 108 Water Step Aerobics	HESS 243 Bowling	HESD 273 Jazz Dance
HESF 109 Step Aerobics	HESS 245 Golf	HESD 274 Modern Dance I
HESF 110 Adapted Physical Education	HESS 246 Handball	HESD 275 Modern Dance II
HESF 111 Indoor Group Cycling	HESR 248 Squash	HESO 276 Whitewater Rafting
HESA 214 Beginning Swimming	HESR 249 Tennis I	HESO 277 Mountain Biking
HESA 215 Advanced Beginning Swimming	HESR 250 Tennis II	HESO 278 Fly Fishing
	HESS 251 Archery	HESF 279 Yoga I
HEST 216 Soccer	HESS 252 Skiing/Snowboarding	HESF 280 Yoga II
HESA 217 Survival Swimming	HESO 253 Orienteering	HESO 281 Introduction to Challenge Course Programming
HESS 219 Gymnastics	HESS 254 Beginning Equitation	
HESA 221 Intermediate Swimming	HESO 255 Basic Canoeing	HESF 282 Advanced Aerobics and Leadership
HESA 223 Lifeguard Training	HESR 256 Racquetball	
HESA 224 Water Safety Instructor	HESO 257 Backpacking	HESO 283 Mountaineering
HESA 226 Skin and Scuba Diving I	HESO 258 Basic Rock Climbing	HESO 284 Sea Kayaking
HESA 227 Scuba Diving II	HESO 259 Intermediate Rock Climbing	HESS 295 Special Topics in Physical Education
HESA 229 Scuba Leadership	HESS 260 Intermediate Equitation	
HESF 230 Pilates/Core Training	HEST 261 Basketball	HESS 296 Independent Study in Physical Education

COACHING EDUCATION

HESM 201 Coaching Baseball/Softball	HESM 207 Coaching Tennis	HESM 301 Coaching Practicum
HESM 202 Coaching Basketball	HESM 208 Coaching Track & Field/ Cross-Country	HESM 381 Athletic Training
HESM 203 Coaching Football		HESM 477 Coaching Concepts
HESM 204 Coaching Golf	HESM 209 Coaching Volleyball	HESM 478 Principles of Sport Science
HESM 205 Coaching Soccer	HESM 211 Coaching Strength Training and Conditioning	HESM 479 Sport Management
HESM 206 Coaching Swimming and Diving		

SPORTS SCIENCE

HESM 314 Methods of Group Exercise Instruction	HESM 303 Sports Science Practicum	HESM 480 Principles of Exercise Programming

HEALTH

HESM 212 Alcohol, Drugs, and Tobacco	HESM 286 Nutrition, Exercise, and Weight Control	HESM 335 Prevention of Sexual Assault and Violence
HESM 213 Human Sexuality		
HESM 280 Responding to Emergencies	HESM 287 Stress Management	HESM 375 Health Planning and Programming
HESM 281 First Responder	HESM 300 Practicum in Health	
HESM 284 Women's Health Issues	NTR 301 Introduction to Human Nutrition	HESM 377 Methods of Health Promotion
HESM 285 Personal Health		

OUTDOOR LEADERSHIP

HESM/PRTM 214 Introduction to Adventure Education	HESM 216 Backcountry Instruction Methodology	HESM 302 Practicum Experience in Outdoor Programs
HESM/PRTM 215 Principles and Practices of Outdoor Leadership		

DISTANCE EDUCATION

HESF 101 Health and Wellness	HESS 239 Self Defense	HESM 381 Athletic Training
HESF 102 Fitness Walking	HESS 243 Bowling	HESM 477 Coaching Concepts
HESF 104 Swim Conditioning	HESS 245 Golf	HESM 478 Exercise Physiology and Sports Science
HESF 105 Aerobics and Body Conditioning	HESR 249 Tennis I	
	HESO 277 Mountain Biking	HESM 479 Sport Management
HESF 107 Run Conditioning	HESF 279 Yoga I	HESM 284 Women's Health Issues
HESF 109 Step Aerobics	HESF 282 Advanced Aerobics and Leadership	HESM 285 Personal Health
HESA 221 Intermediate Swimming		HESM 286 Nutrition, Exercise, and Weight Management
HESF 230 Pilates/Core Training	HESM 202 Coaching Basketball	
HESF 237 Weight Training	HESM 211 Strength Training and Conditioning	

Table of Contents

SECTION 1: GOAL SETTING

Chapter 1.

SECTION 2: HEALTH-RELATED FITNESS

Chapter 2.

Chapter 3.

Chapter 4.

Chapter 5.

SECTION 3: WELLNESS

Chapter 6.

Chapter 7.

Chapter 8.

SECTION 4: SPECIAL TOPICS

Chapter 9.

Chapter 10.

Chapter 11.

Chapter 12.

Preface

Many years ago, the faculty of the NC State Department of Physical Education, now the Department of Health and Exercise Studies, realized a need for a health/fitness textbook that was tailored for our students. Our department offers a comprehensive Basic Instruction Program (B.I.P.) that includes over 100 different health/fitness and skill classes. The challenge was to find (or in this case create) a textbook that could be used by many of these classes that encompassed uniform course objectives and learning outcomes while simultaneously allowing for differences in teaching methodology and skill requirements.

Much time and effort was put into the creation of *Focus on Fitness and Wellness* and our students have benefited from its inclusion in our instruction. After several editions and multiple changes in our content, we believe our current version gives instructors and students a textbook that provides all the materials necessary to reach our department's core course objectives and learning outcomes for health/fitness classes.

Objectives for Courses
in the Category of Health and Exercise Studies

Each course in the Health and Exercise Studies category of the university's *General Education Program* will provide instruction and guidance that help students to:

1. Acquire the fundamentals of health-related fitness, encompassing cardiorespiratory and cardiovascular endurance, muscular strength and endurance, muscular flexibility and body composition;

2. Apply knowledge of the fundamentals of health-related fitness toward developing, maintaining, and sustaining an active and healthy lifestyle;

3. Acquire or enhance the basic motor skills and skill-related competencies, concepts, and strategies used in physical activities and sport; and

4. Gain a thorough working knowledge, appreciation, and understanding of the spirit and rules, history, safety, and etiquette of physical activities and sport.

Student Learning Outcomes

By the end of this course, students will be able to:

1. Explain and perform the fitness requirements associated with this class including cardiorespiratory and cardiovascular endurance, muscular strength and endurance, muscular flexibility and body composition.

2. Perform fitness activities through in-class and out-of-class activities.

3. Discuss and explain how adopting healthy lifestyle practices will lead to lifelong wellness.

4. Identify and explain how the body responds during physical activity.

5. Explain how utilizing different types of equipment, environment, and principles of training affect the intensity of an individual's workout.

6. Identify the risks associated with this class and other fitness activities.

7. Demonstrate ability and knowledge of specific aerobic movements.

8. Demonstrate and safely perform activities associated with this class.

This "in-house" specialty production has progressed into a quality textbook that will be utilized in various school settings across the nation.

Acknowledgments

Special thanks to the listed faculty members who assumed the role of Chapter Editor in coordinating updates and changes for this edition. Special thanks to Beth Fath for coordinating the update of photos for Chapter 4—Flexibility.

I would also like to thank Tim Winslow for being the Department Editor for 14 years, as well as Debbie Williamson and Heather Tatreau for their previous editorial contributions.

Peter Koutroumpis,
Department Managing Editor

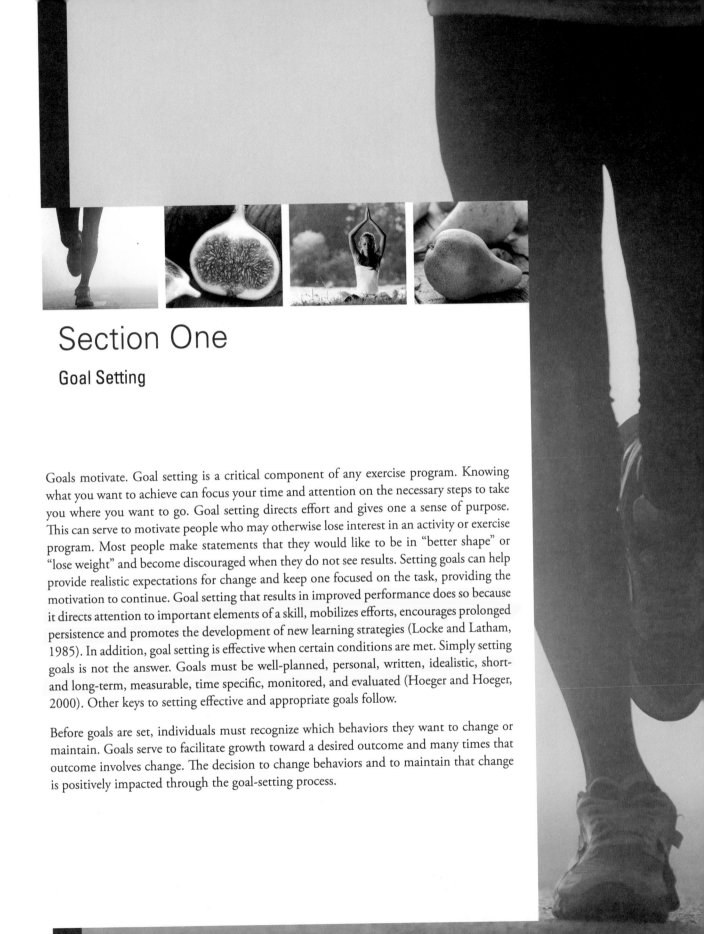

Section One

Goal Setting

Goals motivate. Goal setting is a critical component of any exercise program. Knowing what you want to achieve can focus your time and attention on the necessary steps to take you where you want to go. Goal setting directs effort and gives one a sense of purpose. This can serve to motivate people who may otherwise lose interest in an activity or exercise program. Most people make statements that they would like to be in "better shape" or "lose weight" and become discouraged when they do not see results. Setting goals can help provide realistic expectations for change and keep one focused on the task, providing the motivation to continue. Goal setting that results in improved performance does so because it directs attention to important elements of a skill, mobilizes efforts, encourages prolonged persistence and promotes the development of new learning strategies (Locke and Latham, 1985). In addition, goal setting is effective when certain conditions are met. Simply setting goals is not the answer. Goals must be well-planned, personal, written, idealistic, short- and long-term, measurable, time specific, monitored, and evaluated (Hoeger and Hoeger, 2000). Other keys to setting effective and appropriate goals follow.

Before goals are set, individuals must recognize which behaviors they want to change or maintain. Goals serve to facilitate growth toward a desired outcome and many times that outcome involves change. The decision to change behaviors and to maintain that change is positively impacted through the goal-setting process.

chapter 1

Goal Setting
Getting Started

by Peggy S. Domingue, M. Ed.

Behavior Change

The need for goal setting is many times a result of a need to change certain behaviors or habits. Behavioral change progresses over time and through stages. Prochaska's Stages of Change (Prochaska, 1994) indicate that individuals proceed through six consistent stages of change. These stages of change are as follows:

Table 1-1. Prochaska's Stages of Change

PRECONTEMPLATION	Thinking about making a change, but decide it is too difficult and avoid doing it.
CONTEMPLATION	Have a desire to change but unsure how to go about making a change.
PREPARATION	Change appears to be possible and plans are made to make a change. This is likely a stage where goals are made.
ACTION	Have made and sustained change(s) for about six months.
MAINTENANCE	Continue to practice new habits successfully for at least one year.
TERMINATION	New habits have been established and efforts to change are complete.

1
___
Chapter
One

Seven Key Steps to Effective Goal Setting

Locke and Latham (1990) propose a seven-step process to maximize the effectiveness of goal setting.

1. **Set appropriate goals.**
    The first step in setting appropriate goals is to assess needs. Before goals can be set, one needs to know what the needs are. In addition, the function of the goal needs to be defined. Knowing the focus of the goal, the type of goal, and the goal difficulty will aid in setting appropriate goals.

2. **Develop goal commitment.**
    People need to be committed to goal achievement. Goal achievement can be enhanced when people participate in the goal setting process, when social support is provided, and rewards for goal achievement are available.

3. **Evaluate barriers to goal attainment.**
    Potential barriers to goal attainment need to be identified. Afterward, strategies on how to overcome these barriers are necessary.

4. **Construct an action plan.**
    Setting goals without having a plan on how to implement them is a plan to fail. Goal setters must put an action plan in place for their goals to be effective. Knowing how to get to where you are going is critical. An action plan tells you how to get where you want to go.

5. **Obtain feedback.**
    Feedback that contains information about how one is progressing toward goals is an important step to effective goal setting. Feedback can come from several sources. One possible source of feedback is the method of evaluation an individual chooses when goals are initially established.

6. **Evaluate goal attainment.**
    Goal attainment and increased motivation is more likely when goals are periodically evaluated. A method of evaluation must be established when goals are set. There should be an organized method to evaluate where one is as they work toward their goals.

7. **Reinforce goal achievement.**
    Goal setters are encouraged to repeat the goal-setting process regardless of whether or not a goal was reached. Setting new goals enhances motivation and increases goal attainment.

Principles of Goal Setting

There are several goal-setting principles throughout the literature. The following principles are commonly found to be important components for a successful goal-setting program (Weinberg and Gould, 2003).

Set Specific Goals
To simply set out to "do-your-best" is not enough when change is necessary. Goals should be specific and measurable and stated in terms that are very well-defined. Setting specific goals are most effective and easy to track and measure.

Set Moderately Difficult but Realistic Goals
Goals that are difficult enough to be challenging, but realistic enough to be achieved are the most effective goals. When goals are too difficult, frustration and a lack of confidence can result. On the other hand, goals that are very easily attained are generally of little value.

Set Short- and Long-term Goals
Both short-term and long-term goals are important and must be set. In addition, short- and long-term goals must be linked to each other. Goals should progress logically according to predetermined objectives. Being able to meet short-term goals that lead to long-term goals can stimulate confidence and motivation.

Set Performance and Process, as Well as Outcome, Goals
Performance goals focus on achieving certain successes based on an individual's previous performance. With performance goals, one is more concerned with making comparisons with one's self and not with other people. Performance goals measure one's progress against one's self regardless of what others are doing or have done. Process goals, on the other hand, focus the attention on criteria

that must be met during the performance so that performance goals can be met. Correctly executing an exercise (process goal) can result in the ability to lift more weight or run a longer distance (performance goal) thus winning a competition or race (outcome goal). Outcome goals focus on the result of an event and can create motivation to succeed on process and performance goals. However, too much focus on outcome goals can create anxiety.

Set Practice and Competition Goals

When an individual chooses to compete, goals for practice and competition must be set. For most, more time is spent practicing for a competition and having specific goals for that practice time can help maintain motivation. Practice goals should complement competition goals so that goals are more likely to be achieved.

Record Goals

Goals should be recorded and posted. The method of recording is whatever one determines to be most practical. The purpose is to be reminded of set goals, focus on those goals, and promote accountability.

Develop Goal Achievement Strategies

Goal achievement strategies should indicate specifically how much, how often, how many, etc. The purpose of developing goal achievement strategies is to define specifically how a goal is to be achieved. This is similar to constructing the action plan mentioned above.

Consider the Participant's Personality and Motivation

Knowing one's self will help determine how to set goals. For some, time restraints and schedules affect the method of how goals are to be achieved or maintained. Personality characteristics can also affect the structure and intensity of goal-setting efforts.

Foster an Individual's Goal Commitment

As mentioned earlier under the seven steps to effective goal setting, one must be committed to a goal before they can hope to achieve it. When people are allowed to set their own goals they take ownership in that goal and are more committed to it.

Provide Goal Support

Enlisting the support of significant others makes goal setting more effective. Educating those around you about your goals and the efforts you are making to achieve them can encourage support. This support is very important in progressing toward goals.

Provide Evaluation of and Feedback about Goals

When goals are set there must be a method put in place to evaluate those goals. This is done at the start of the goal-setting process. Being able to adequately measure progress can provide feedback. This feedback must contain specific information relative to the progress, or lack thereof, in the effort to reach defined goals. Evaluation is critical and can provide the information needed to alter goals.

Common Problems in Goal Setting

The following are common problems often found in goal setting (Weinberg and Gould, 2003; Cox, 2007):

Poorly Written Goals

Goals should be written so they are specific, measurable, achievable, realistic, and timely (SMART). When goals are vague, lack direction, cannot be measured, and are unrealistic people are not motivated to strive to attain them. There is no motivation to attain goals that have no purpose or intent to change behavior. Writing goals in a specific manner will serve to motivate and facilitate change.

Setting Too Many Goals Too Soon

People anxious to see change many times set too many goals too soon and become discouraged. A few realistic goals are better than several unrealistic goals. Having the time to realistically implement and monitor set goals is important to the effectiveness of goal setting.

Failure to Devise a Strategy

One of the goal-setting principles is to develop a goal-setting strategy or action plan. The purpose of this strategy is to plan how one will achieve this goal. Not having a strategy or plan on how to achieve a goal results in certain failure for the goal-setting process.

Failure to Monitor Progress

Knowing where one is in the process of attaining a goal is critical to not only achieving the goal, but also staying motivated to attain the goal. Well-defined goals can be easily monitored. Having the ability to monitor progress will allow necessary adjustments to be made and will provide direction for future efforts.

Failing to Adjust Goals

Being aware of the possibility that goals may need to be adjusted can eliminate disappointment when changes need to be made.

Not Planning for Evaluation

When evaluation is planned for, then one understands that periodic evaluation will occur and the effort to stay on task is encouraged. The lack of evaluation is a major reason for failure in goal-setting programs. When there is no follow-up, there is no way to assess progress.

Steps to Designing a Goal-Setting System

The following are three basic steps to design a goal-setting system:

Preparation and Planning

Before setting goals one must assess abilities and needs. An integral part of assessment is identifying areas that need improvement or change. When needed changes are identified, a plan for how to achieve that change begins to take shape. Using the seven steps to effective goal setting and the principles of goal setting will provide direction on setting goals and formulating a plan to achieve them.

Set Appropriate Goals

As mentioned earlier, goals must be challenging but realistic. They must be well-planned, personal, written, realistic, short- and long-term, measurable, time specific, monitored, and evaluated (Hoeger and Hoeger, 2000). What is appropriate for one person may not be appropriate for another. Setting the appropriate goals is the foundation for meeting those goals.

Evaluate Goals

From the start, a plan on how to evaluate the goals you set must be established. When the goal is set, there should be an evaluation plan that corresponds to that goal. Knowing that there will be an evaluation motivates one to stay on task. Accurate evaluations provide necessary information so that one knows if and when to adjust goals along the way. More importantly, evaluating goals and progress toward a goal makes the probability of achieving that goal a reality.

Example of a specific goal, planned and written in a format that will allow for evaluation of success.

LONG-TERM GOAL	I want to lose 10 pounds, measured by a body weight scale, in the next 2 months by doing 30 minutes of cardio a day, weight training 3×/wk, and following a healthy diet plan which I will monitor by using a goal chart.						
SHORT-TERM GOALS	Week 1						
	Day 1	Day 2	Day 3	Day 4	Day 5	Day 6	Day 7
Cardio exercise for 30 minutes per day at 70% of THR							
Weight training a minimum of 3 days							
Eat 2300 calories or less per day							
Do not eat after 9 pm each day							
Drink eight 8 oz. glasses of water per day							

A blank chart to write out your personal goal for the semester.

LONG-TERM GOAL							
SHORT-TERM GOALS	Week 1						
	Day 1	Day 2	Day 3	Day 4	Day 5	Day 6	Day 7

Summary Questions

1. Think of one health behavior you would like to change. List Prochaska's Stages of Change and decide which one applies to your target behavior.

2. Describe eleven commonly found components in a successful goal-setting program.

3. Summarize six common problems in goal setting.

4. Identify methods of behavior change, barriers to change, stressors, and indicators of relapse.

Web Sites

http://www.goal-setting-guide.com/smart-goals.html

http://www.mindtools.com/page6.html

References

Bridges, W. (2004). *Transitions: Making sense of life's changes.* Cambridge, MA: Da Dapo Press.

Hoeger, Werner, & Sharon A. Hoeger. (2000). *Lifetime Physical Fitness and Wellness,* Sixth Edition. Englewood, CO 80110: Morton Publishing Company.

Locke, E.A., & Latham, G.P. (1985). The application of goal setting to sports. *Journal of Sport Psychology,* 7, 205–222.

Locke, E.A., & Latham, G.P. (1990). *A theory of goal setting and task performance.* Englewood Cliffs, NJ: Prentice Hall.

Prochaska, J.O.; Norcross, J.C.; Clemente C.C. (1994) *Changing for Good.* New York: William Morrow and Company.

Weinberg, Robert S. PhD., & Daniel Gould, PhD. (2003). *Foundation of Sport and Exercise Psychology,* Third Edition. P.O. Box 5076, Champaign, IL 61825–5076: *Human Kinetics.*

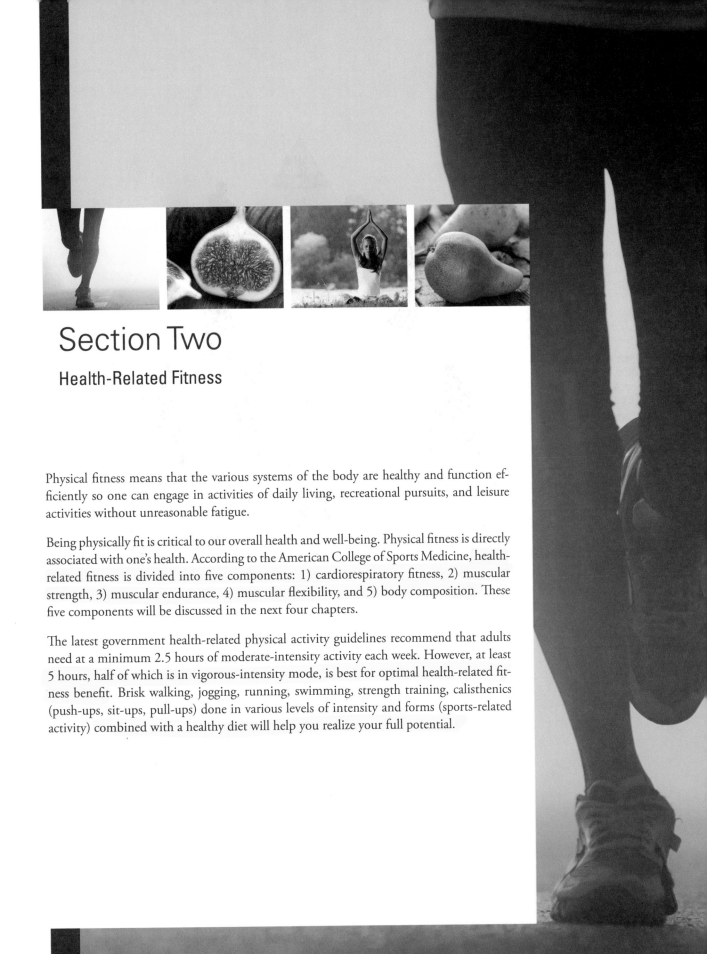

Section Two

Health-Related Fitness

Physical fitness means that the various systems of the body are healthy and function efficiently so one can engage in activities of daily living, recreational pursuits, and leisure activities without unreasonable fatigue.

Being physically fit is critical to our overall health and well-being. Physical fitness is directly associated with one's health. According to the American College of Sports Medicine, health-related fitness is divided into five components: 1) cardiorespiratory fitness, 2) muscular strength, 3) muscular endurance, 4) muscular flexibility, and 5) body composition. These five components will be discussed in the next four chapters.

The latest government health-related physical activity guidelines recommend that adults need at a minimum 2.5 hours of moderate-intensity activity each week. However, at least 5 hours, half of which is in vigorous-intensity mode, is best for optimal health-related fitness benefit. Brisk walking, jogging, running, swimming, strength training, calisthenics (push-ups, sit-ups, pull-ups) done in various levels of intensity and forms (sports-related activity) combined with a healthy diet will help you realize your full potential.

If you're inactive (rarely active)
increase daily activities at the base of the pyramid.

- Walk whenever you can.
- Make leisure time as active as possible.

If you're sporadic (active some of the time, but not regularly)
increase daily activities in the middle of the pyramid.

- Plan activity in your day.
- Set realistic goals.

If you're consistent (active most days of the week)
choose activities from all levels of the pyramid.

- Change your routine if you start to get bored.
- Explore new activities.

CUT DOWN ON
sitting • watching TV • working or playing at the computer

3+ TIMES A WEEK
Stretch & strengthen your muscles
take stretch breaks • do yoga/tai chi • lift weights • use tension bands • do push-ups and curl-ups

3–4 TIMES A WEEK
Give your heart and lungs a workout
bike • hike • run/jog • swim • do water aerobics • walk briskly • play basketball • in-line skate

EVERYDAY
Walk often & stay active
walk your dog • do yardwork • play golf • go bowling • park your car farther away • take the stairs instead of the elevator

©Hayden-McNeil, LLC

chapter 2

Health-Related Fitness
Cardiorespiratory Fitness

by Nita Horne, MS; Paul Powers, MS

Cardiorespiratory Fitness

Cardiorespiratory fitness is the ability to perform moderate to high intensity dynamic exercise involving large muscle groups for prolonged periods of time. It is sometimes referred to as cardiorespiratory endurance, aerobic fitness, or aerobic capacity. The body's circulatory and respiratory systems function together to supply oxygen to the working muscles to produce energy. It is the efficiency with which the body is able to transport, absorb and use oxygen during exercise that is measured to determine one's level of cardiorespiratory fitness.

Improved Cardiorespiratory Fitness

To improve one's cardiorespiratory fitness, an individual needs to engage in activities that place an added demand, or overload, on the circulatory and respiratory systems at intensities that result in physiological adaptations. These adaptations enable the muscles to produce and use more energy during exercise and therefore the muscles can work more intensely and for a longer duration. Here are just some of the physiological adaptations and health benefits from improved cardiorespiratory fitness.

2

Chapter
Two

PHYSIOLOGICAL ADAPTATIONS	
Increased	**Decreased**
• Heart volume • Resting and maximum stroke volume • Maximum cardiac output • Total blood volume • Lactate threshold • Maximal ventilation • Maximum oxygen consumption • Capillary density to exercised muscles • Mobilization and utilization of fat • Insulin sensitivity	• Resting heart rate

HEALTH BENEFITS	
Increased	**Decreased**
• Aerobic work capacity • HDL ("good") cholesterol • Heart function • Immune function • Sense of well-being	• Fatigue in daily activities • Body fat stores • Risk for Type-2 diabetes • Blood pressure to normal levels • Risk of certain cancers • Risk of mortality from all causes • Rate of osteoporosis • Symptoms of anxiety/tension/depression

Types of Activities to Improve Cardiorespiratory Fitness

The American College of Sports Medicine (ACSM) places cardiorespiratory activities into three groups categorized according to skill demands.

	SKILL DEMANDS	CARDIORESPIRATORY ACTIVITIES	TRAINING EFFECT ON CARDIORESPIRATORY FITNESS
Group 1	Require very little skill and provide a constant intensity level.	Jogging, running, walking, cardio equipment	Generally the most ideal for maintenance and improvement of cardiorespiratory fitness.
Group 2	Require more skill than Group 1 activities. The intensity is dependent on the skill of the individual.	Swimming, aerobic dance, cycling on a real bicycle (not a stationary bike), skating, skiing	Can be as effective as Group 1 activities for maintenance and improvement of cardiorespiratory fitness provided that the individual exercising is skilled enough in that activity to maintain the minimum exercise intensity.
Group 3	Incorporates a large variety of skill requirements and intensity levels. Generally more fun than activities in Groups 1 and 2 and are good ways to make cardiorespiratory fitness more enjoyable.	Basketball, soccer, racket sports	Mostly effective for maintenance of cardiorespiratory fitness rather than improvement since there is less control over the intensity levels.

Exercise Prescription for Cardiorespiratory Fitness

Much like a drug prescription for an illness, exercise can be prescribed in varying dosages. The exercise dose, or quantity and intensity of exercise needed for the desired effect, will vary depending on the desired response. The interaction of the variables frequency, intensity, duration and type of activity all determine the dose of exercise. This is called the FITT principle and is used to establish an individualized exercise prescription.

Table 2-1. Cardiorespiratory Fitness Guidelines (ACSM, 2011) The American College of Sports Medicine (ACSM) recommends the following exercise prescription to improve and maintain cardiorespiratory fitness (for apparently healthy adults of all ages).

FITT PRINCIPLE	MODERATE INTENSITY EXERCISE	VIGOROUS INTENSITY EXERCISE	COMBINED	WEIGHT LOSS
Frequency: How Often (days per week)	≥ 5×/week	≥ 3×/week	3–5×/week	5–7×/week
Intensity: How Hard (load/resistance)	50–60% HRR, 60–75% MHR	≥ 60% HRR	Moderate or Vigorous	Moderate
Time: How Long (length of training session)	≥ 30 min/day	≥ 20 min/day	≥ 20 min/day	50–60 min/day
Type: Aerobic or Anaerobic Exercise	Aerobic	Aerobic	Aerobic	Aerobic
Volume: Accumulated Total of Activity	≥ 150 min/week	≥ 75 min/week	≥ 75 min/week	300 min/week

- Intermittent activities in 10-minute sessions have the same health benefits as continuous activities (but not necessarily the same fitness benefits).

- Adults engaging in competitive sports or activities with higher fitness demands can benefit from more advanced training than the ACSM exercise prescription for cardiorespiratory fitness.

AEROBIC AND ANAEROBIC ACTIVITIES DEFINED

- **Aerobic Activities**—Use large muscle groups in a rhythmic, continuous manner, keeping heart rate consistently elevated for an extended period of time. The intensity allows the body to supply enough oxygen for the activity to continue for long periods. Jogging, lap swimming, fitness walking.
- **Aerobic Activities**—Explosive, start-and-stop activities in which the heart rate fluctuates. Intensity is so great that the body is unable to deliver the oxygen that is demanded of the activity for it to continue for long periods. Weight training, sprinting activities, most sports.

AEROBIC AND ANAEROBIC ENERGY SYSTEMS DEFINED

The body needs energy to perform physical activities. The energy is supplied to the body through one of three energy systems, which are either aerobic or anaerobic.

1. Aerobic system
2. Lactate anaerobic system
3. Phosphate anaerobic system

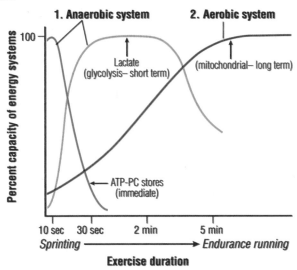

FIGURE 2-1. With an overlap of energy systems, the anaerobic system provides the working muscles with ATP from ATP–PC stores and the lactate or glycolysis path. The aerobic system provides ATP from mitochondria which require oxygen to burn carbohydrates and fats.

The shift between energy systems depends on the intensity and the duration of an activity. Short, intense bursts of exercise rely mainly on the anaerobic systems while lower intensity longer durations of exercise use mostly the aerobic system.

The three substrates of stored carbohydrates (glycogen), fat, and protein (breakdown of muscle tissue) contribute varying percentages during different intensities of these three energy systems.

Energy Substrate	At Rest	Light-to-Moderate Intensity Exercise	High-Intensity Endurance Exercise	High-Intensity Sprint-Type Exercise
Protein	2–5%	2–5%	5–8%	2%
Carbohydrate	35%	40%	70%	95%
Fat	60%	55%	15%	3%

Note: For fat loss, Calories burned is the key—not the energy substrate used; otherwise, "At Rest" would seem to be the best intensity to lose fat which is not true. The highest Calorie burn for the same duration would be high-intensity sprint-type exercise which burns the least fat.

Training Zones

The Training Zones designated here represent the shift between energy systems and different intensities. Different training intensities lead to different physiological training adaptations in the body, so to improve overall cardiorespiratory fitness, it is important to vary the intensity either within the same exercise session or for different workouts during the week.

	% OF MAX HR	KARVONEN MODIFIED	VO2 MAX	RPE SCALE
Zone 1 (Recovery, aerobic)	87–105 50%–60% MHR	117–129 50%–60% HRR		2–4
Zone 2 (Endurance, aerobic)	105–122 60%–70% MHR	129–140 60%–70% HRR		4–5
Zone 3 (Stamina, aerobic)	122–140 70%–80% MHR	140–152 70%–80% HRR	60–65% VO2 max	5–7
Zone 4 (Economy, anaerobic)	140–157 80%–90% MHR	152–163 80%–90% HRR	80% VO2 max	7–9
Zone 5 (Speed, anaerobic)	157–175 90%–100% MHR	163–175 90%–100% HRR	100% VO2 max	9–10
Max HR	175	175	>100%	10

Zone 1: Comfortable and easy, warmup
Zone 2: Challenging but comfortable
Zone 3: Aerobic zone, challenging and uncomfortable
Zone 4: Anaerobic Threshold Zone, breathless—not maximum—but winded
Zone 5: Redline Zone, used mostly during interval training

Methods to Assess Intensity of Cardiorespiratory Activities

While engaging in a cardiorespiratory activity, how can intensity be assessed by the exerciser? Here are a few common methods used to assess intensity.

COMMON METHODS TO ASSESS INTENSITY

1) RPE—Rating of Perceived Exertion

A simple method for an exerciser to assess intensity during cardiorespiratory activity is by monitoring how his/her body feels during exercise. This is subjective with the exerciser "perceiving" his/her exertion. By focusing on bodily sensations such as increased breathing rate, increased heart rate, sweating, muscle fatigue and appraising these together as an overall feeling of exertion, the exerciser can increase or decrease effort to adjust intensity of the activity. The Borg Scale (Borg, 1982) and RPE Scale (Modified Borg RPE) provides more guidance to assess intensity. These scales have been validated against measures of heart rate.

Some findings from studies on the RPE Scale are as follows:

- Men tend to underestimate initially until more familiar with the scale.
- Women tend to overestimate initially until more familiar with the scale.
- Athletes often misinterpret the scale by not focusing on overall effort but on muscle fatigue.
- There is a significant learning curve for the exerciser, but after becoming more familiar with the scale, values deviate toward the mean.

RPE is useful when heart rate cannot be measured accurately, such as when medications affect heart rate.

BORG SCALE 6–20	RPE SCALE 0–10 MODIFIED BORG SCALE
6	0 Nothing at all
7 Very, very light	0.5 Very, very weak
8	1 Very weak
9 Very light	2 Weak
10	3 Moderate
11 Fairly light	4 Somewhat strong
12	5 Strong
13 Somewhat hard	6
14	7 Very strong
15 Hard	8
16	9
17 Very hard	10 Very, very strong
18	*Maximal
19 Very, very hard	
20	

2) Heart Rate

Another measure commonly used to assess intensity during cardiorespiratory activity is monitoring heart rate.

When Should the Heart Rate Count be Taken?

- **Resting Heart Rate**—A "true" resting heart rate is taken in the morning before rising from bed. The count should be for a full minute. After rising, the heart rate will increase possibly 10–20 beats per minute. If awakened by an alarm clock, the count can still be taken after resting quietly for several minutes.

- Fluctuations in heart rate may be due to: lack of sleep, medications, emotional stress, hydration level, food intake, caffeine, illness, environmental temperature, or humidity.

- **Exercise Heart Rate**—Most exercisers take a heart rate count immediately post-exercise, but there are reasons to take the heart rate count at other times: pre-exercise, during exercise, immediately post-exercise, and within a few minutes post-exercise.

  1. Pre-exercise—This count provides a relative base to compare the exercise heart rate. An unusually high pre-exercise heart rate may be due to one of the factors listed above for "fluctuations."

  2. During exercise—The heart rate will plateau (rise during the warm-up and stay consistent through the aerobic phase, then drop during the cooldown); therefore, if the intensity remains the same, it will not matter when during the aerobic phase of the workout that the heart rate is counted.

  3. Immediately post-exercise—The post-exercise heart rate will be consistent with the aerobic phase heart rate, right before starting the cooldown. The heart rate needs to be counted within 15 seconds of reducing the activity level. After this, the heart rate will slow down (due to decreased activity and decreased need for oxygenated blood to the working muscles), entering a recovery phase.

  4. A few minutes post-exercise—This recovery heart rate can be an indicator of fitness level. The more fit individual will have a faster recovery in returning to the pre-exercise heart rate.

How Many Seconds Should the Heart Rate Count Be?

- **Resting Heart Rate**—60 seconds
- **Exercise Heart Rate**—10 seconds preferred (× 6 = beats per minute). Within 15 seconds of reducing the intensity of exercise, the heart rate will begin to slow down; therefore, a longer count would be inaccurate due to the heart rate lowering. (Note: Some people prefer a 6-second count, because the exerciser only needs to add a "zero" to the count to have the beats per minute count. This is fine, but the concern is that if a beat or two is missed, it is then magnified by ten. For example, a 6-second heart rate count of 12 = 120 beats per minute. If one beat was missed, it actually should be 13 = 130 bpm or two missed beats, 14 = 140 bpm. This is a significant difference.)

What is a "Good" Resting Heart Rate?

Resting heart rate will vary greatly among individuals and is primarily dependent upon age and fitness level. Check the table below for resting heart rate norms.

YMCA Norms for Resting Heart Rate (beats/min)

AGE (YEAR)	18–25		26–35		36–45		46–55	
GENDER	M	F	M	F	M	F	M	F
Excellent	49–55	54–60	49–54	54–59	50–56	54–59	50–57	54–60
Good	57–61	61–65	57–61	60–64	60–62	62–64	59–63	61–65
Above Average	63–65	66–69	62–65	66–68	64–66	66–69	64–67	66–69
Average	67–69	70–73	66–70	69–71	68–70	70–72	68–71	70–73
Below Average	71–73	74–78	72–74	72–76	73–76	74–78	73–76	74–77
Poor	76–81	80–84	77–81	78–82	77–82	79–82	79–83	78–84
Very Poor	84–95	86–100	84–94	84–94	86–96	84–92	85–97	85–96

Adapted from: YMCA. *Y's way to fitness.* (3rd.Ed.) as printed in Nieman (1995). Reprinted with permission from the YMCA of the USA.

For Target Heart Rate Zone calculation, see Karvonen Formula (page 23).

For a simple prediction of maximum heart rate, here are some calculations.

1. MHR = 220 – age   *Note: These are just a few of the many different predictive equations.
2. Men: MHR = 214 – (0.8 × age)   Women: MHR = 209 – (0.9 × age)   Multiply by intensity %
3. Men: MHR = 214 – age   Women: MHR= 209 – age   Multiply by intensity %

How To Assess Heart Rates

An exerciser can count his/her pulse by using the index and middle fingers of one hand (the thumb has its own pulse and should not be used) at an artery site. The most common sites for assessing pulse where arteries lie close to the surface of the skin are the radial artery (found on the wrist, thumb-side) and the carotid (found in the groove on the neck to the side of the larynx). The fingers should be pressed lightly at the carotid artery because pressing too hard may shut off some of the blood supply to the brain causing light headedness. Another concern is that the carotid artery has baroreceptors that will signal the brain to slow the heart rate if the fingers press too firmly and this could also result in the exerciser becoming lightheaded or even losing consciousness.

Monitors

There are many varieties of heart rate monitors, wrist bands, and sport watches that can provide real-time heart rate readings. A common design has electrodes detecting the heart beat and transmitting the signal to a wristwatch for the exerciser to view. A more recent design has LED technology detecting blood flow and transmitting this information to a wrist band that interprets the heart rate. Many of these monitors have additional features such as stopwatch functions, setting of target heart rate zones, recording splits, GPS, and connectivity for online analysis and graphs of activity and heart rates over time.

3) VO2 max

VO2 max or volume of maximal oxygen consumption is a common measure used to assess cardiorespiratory fitness. VO2 max is determined by the cardiac output (the maximal amount of blood the heart pumps per minute) and the arterial-venous oxygen difference (the amount of oxygen utilized by the exercising muscles). As exercise intensity increases, the volume of both oxygen consumed and carbon dioxide exhaled also increase. With VO2 there is a maximum level of oxygen consumption the exerciser will reach and not exceed even with increased exercise intensity. Since VO2 max is the measure of the body's ability to use oxygen to generate energy, training zones for the exerciser can be based on this measure.

Stress Tests

The most accurate method to assess cardiorespiratory fitness is to conduct a maximal stress test in a laboratory with a protocol usually for a treadmill or stationary bike. VO2 max is measured with the exerciser completing the test to exhaustion or some designated endpoint. This requires trained personnel to properly monitor the test (sometimes a physician if concerns for cardiac arrest; also ECG electrodes placed on the exerciser's chest to monitor heart rate) and requires expensive equipment for gas exchange analysis. The exerciser breathes through a mouthpiece with inhalations and exhalations being captured. The amount of carbon dioxide exhaled at maximum energy output provides a measure of how much oxygen the exerciser is burning, thus converting into energy = VO2 max. Also, the heart rate values from the ECG readings in the stress test matched to rating of perceived exertion (RPE) provide valuable information about the cardiorespiratory fitness of the exerciser.

Submaximal Tests

There are simpler ways than a stress test to approximate VO2 max. Submaximal testing generally uses a treadmill or bike protocol in which heart rate response can be determined by one or more workloads during the test and then VO2 max can be predicted. The accuracy of the VO2 max prediction can be affected by factors affecting the exerciser's heart rate (anxiety, caffeine, medication), by the ability of the exerciser to maintain the testing pace, by the mechanical efficiency of the exerciser with the testing activity, and due to variation of maximal heart rates at given ages.

Other submaximal testing involves measuring performance (Rockport Walk Test, Step Test, Balke Test) of a specific distance, acquiring the performance time and exercise heart rates, then using known correlations to predict VO2 max. For running, there is the Balke Test which predicts VO2 max accurate to within ± 5%. The Balke Test involves having the exerciser run around a track for exactly 15 minutes. The aim is to cover the most distance possible, with advice to hold back on the pace for the first five minutes, to run hard for the next five minutes, and to go all out for the last five minutes. The total distance covered in 15 minutes is then converted into VO2 max by using the following formula.

$$\text{VO2 max} = (\text{meters run} \times 0.0115) + 10.4$$

An individual's VO2 max is to a large extent determined by genetic factors, but it can be increased by training. General increases for VO2 max can be between 5% and 20% with even 60% increase being reported. For a small portion of individuals, training seems to make little difference in VO2 max.

4) Pace

To assess cardiorespiratory fitness for many activities (running, swimming, walking), pace is a good measure of effort and thus intensity. Due to GPS watches and having known distances, the calculation of time for a given distance allows goals to be set to attain certain paces.

Intensity Threshold

Is there a threshold intensity of exercise to improve cardiorespiratory fitness? In many studies there is evidence of a minimum threshold of intensity for benefit, but not in all studies. The overload principle of training states that below a minimum intensity or threshold, the body will not be challenged sufficiently to result in increased VO2 max or other physiological adaptations. The lack of consistent findings in these studies for a threshold may be related to the varying initial fitness levels of the subjects and the precise training regimens. For example, well-trained athletes were found to need near maximal (95–100% VO2 max) training intensities to improve, whereas moderately trained athletes improved VO2 max at training intensities of 70–80% VO2 max. Because of varying fitness levels and individual response variability to training, prescriptions for intensity may need to be monitored and adjusted.

Performance Criteria for Cardiorespiratory Fitness Activities

A combination of factors determine an individual's performance in cardiorespiratory activities.

Efficiency of lungs, heart and blood in delivering oxygen through the body (VO2 max) × Efficiency of muscles translating oxygen and fuel into energy (Lactate threshold) × Efficiency of body in translating movement into speed (Economy) = Performance

Training for Cardiorespiratory Fitness

Precautions for Participation in a Cardiorespiratory Fitness Program

Although participation is beneficial to almost everyone, physical limitations need to be identified first. Individuals over age 35 should complete a physical examination and receive clearance from their physician before participating in a fitness program, regardless of health status. Individuals having any medical problems should also complete a physical examination and receive clearance from their physician, regardless of age. Over-training should be avoided by progressing slowly and allowing the body time to recover between exercise sessions. It is important to cease exercising if pain is persistent. Terminate the exercise session and consult a physician if experiencing chest pain, dizziness, shortness of breath, or nausea.

Components of a Cardiorespiratory Exercise Session

The three basic components of a cardiorespiratory exercise session are warm-up, conditioning stimulus, and cooldown.

COMPONENTS	DURATION	CRITERIA
Warm-Up	5–15 minutes Depends upon the age and fitness level of the exerciser (older individuals and those with increased risk of irregular heart events benefit from longer warm-up and cooldown periods).	The warmup represents a period of metabolic and cardiovascular adjustment from rest to exercise. The most appropriate activities for the warm-up are those that are similar to the conditioning stimulus, performed at 50% of the stimulus intensity
Conditioning Stimulus	Duration depends on training goals	FITT Principle
Cooldown	Depends upon the age and fitness level of the exerciser (older individuals and those with increased risk of irregular heart events benefit from longer warm-up and cooldown periods).	The cooldown represents a period of metabolic and cardiovascular adjustment from exercise to rest. To increase flexibility, stretching activities may be appropriate during the cooldown.

Record Keeping

Maintaining a training log has many benefits and allows for personal reflection. Many serious exercisers report that they maintain some kind of training log or activity record. Recordings can be maintained via a calendar, chart, log, a diary format, and with online applications. A training log allows an individual to set goals and monitor progress. The log can be a source of motivation and can provide discipline for the exerciser. The log can enhance awareness of physical capabilities and physiological and psychological changes. A training log can also provide an early warning of overtraining, which can lead to overuse injuries.

Training Variations

The benefits of cardiorespiratory fitness have been identified throughout this chapter. It is important to maintain some variety in your workouts if you wish to elevate your fitness level, prepare to race, or simply avoid the boredom of the same old routine. Ideally, a training schedule will alternate hard and easy days rather than consist of a gradual linear progression. When we think of aerobic exercise we often think of the most used methods of running, walking, cycling, or swimming. However, there are other methods of aerobic activity, which include aerobic and water aerobic classes. All of these activities use the large muscle groups in a rhythmic and continuous manner to keep the heart rate elevated for an extended period of time. Here are "The Big Six" types of training that can help you add some variety to your cardiorespiratory sessions. Specific examples are given for those relevant to your type of activity.

1. Fartlek Training

Fartlek is a Swedish term for "speed play." This "speed play" is just how it sounds—play! The exerciser has complete freedom to structure the workout how he/she chooses. Many runners have "lost" the watch for a day, gone out for a 4–5 mile loop, and gotten involved in speed play by doing pick-ups from one light pole to the next with jog recovery between repetitions. The distance traveled or time involved on the hard phase doesn't always have to be of concern. Although unstructured sessions can allow the exerciser to think and be creative, some may choose to have a well-thought-out fartlek session prior to beginning.

Fartlek training helps to train specific muscle groups and the lungs for a variety of paces.

Here are some examples of a fartlek session for different activities. Remember, "speed play" requires that you maintain the creativity so it is truly "play."

25 Minute Fartlek Run
3 minute jog followed by 4 minute up-tempo pace; then 4 minute jog recovery, 3 minute up-tempo pace; then 3 minute jog recovery, 2 minute up-tempo pace followed by 2 minute recovery, 1 minute fast pace followed by 1 minute jog recovery; 2–3 minute jog cool-down

Fartlek Swim
Following an adequate warm-up session, swimmer will do a 30 minute continuous swim with frequent pace changes; 25 yd easy followed by 25 yd fast swim followed by 25 yd easy; 25 yd sprints could be mixed in but be careful to keep moving during those active recovery phases otherwise it may become an interval session.

2.   Interval Training
These are the most structured of all workouts. Intervals involve repetition training that alternates intense segments ranging from 30 seconds to 5 minutes followed by a recovery period. The following are all positive physiological benefits seen from interval training.

- Improves VO2 Max.

- Helps improve speed.

- Helps improve overall conditioning.

- Helps your body, legs, lungs, and heart adapt to higher demands being placed on them.

- Faster pace is good final race preparation.

Examples for swimmers:
Self-paced Intervals (used in early program training; consist of short distances, easy paces, and liberal recovery times selected by the swimmer)

> *Example*: Swim 50-yd repeats at choice pace; recover until ready for next interval

Strict Intervals (used when intensity of workouts need to be increased; distances remain relatively short, paces become moderate to fast, and recovery times are determined by the pace clock)

> *Example*: Swim 25-yd repeats with a "go time" of :40 (swim time and recovery are included in the :40; each :40 results in a new repeat)

Examples for runners:
6 × 800 meter repeats at 3:00 pace with equal recovery between each interval
3 × 1 mile repeats at 5k race pace with a predetermined amount of recovery between each interval

Examples for cyclists:
10 × 2 minute fast rides with 2 minute recovery between each

Example for fitness walkers:
5 × 30 seconds hard followed by 30 seconds easy; or 5 × 100 m hard/50 m easy

3.   Tempo Work (Runs, Walks, Swims, Rides)
Tempo work is another method used to add intensity to your workout. Tempo could be used as another word for pace. Tempo runs should be faster than your usual training pace. Tempo work is done at a steady intensity close to race pace. These workouts should be tough but not impossible. Tempo work is also known as lactate threshold pace. **Lactate threshold** is the point during exercise at which muscle lactate concentrations increase abruptly. By exercising at nearly race pace your body begins to adapt to exercising at its upper limit. Here are some examples of tempo work for different activities.

For runners:
5 mile run (time-trial) at 10k race pace; or 85–90% of maximum HR

For swimmers:
450 yd time trial swim at high aerobic intensity; 85–90% of max HR

For walkers:
2 mile time trial walk at high aerobic intensity; 85–90% of max HR

For cyclists:
12 mile time trial ride at high aerobic intensity; 85–90% of max HR

4. Hill Work (Resistance)

Hill work or resistance training is another means to add intensity and variety to your training program. Obviously hill work can be done with runners, walkers, and cyclists but is tough to arrange for swimmers.

Here are some benefits for runners, walkers, and cyclists.

- Builds leg strength.

- Makes you better at climbing those hills during race time.

- Enhances speed by building fast twitch muscle fibers.

- Increases both frequency and length of your stride.

- Strengthens the muscles around the knees helping reduce knee injuries.

Example workouts for runners:

5 × 200 meter hill climbs; 4 × 100 meter fast strides (flat surface) after completion; jog recovery; 5 × 200 meter downhill runs; 4 × 100 meter fast strides (flat surface) following downhills; jog recovery

Example for cyclists:

1 hour ride along hilly terrain; or if riding indoors increase resistance and ride at a slower cadence (70 RPM)

Examples for fitness walkers:

4 × uphill/downhill = 5 minutes; could also use bleachers, stairs, or any incline that is substantial distance

Examples for swimmers:

Intervals (repetitions) using paddles; 5 × 100 yd pulls using paddles and buoys to create resistance

5. Long Slow Distance (LSD)

Long distance work does not add intensity to the workout in the same way that the previously mentioned training methods do, but this type of training is essential to the endurance athlete who is looking to build an aerobic fitness base. These longer training sessions help build and maintain stamina. Longer runs (training sessions) also promote cellular adaptations, which improve the cardiovascular system, spares glycogen, and enhances the use of fat as fuel. This type of training could be called "conversational" because you are able to carry on a conversation with others around you in your training group. These longer sessions are done at 60–75% of your maximum HR.

Long is relative to where you are currently in your training program. As a rule of thumb it is a good idea to never exceed 150% of your regular mid-week mileage/yardage. These longer sessions are done once every week, and for some beginning exercisers it is recommended that the LSD be done once every other week. Typically the LSD training day would fit in best on a weekend morning. However, you can make it fit within your training and racing schedule. Remember, these are aerobic sessions, nothing hard!!

Example run:

1 hour moderate run at easy but steady pace; 70% of max HR

Example walk:

1 hour walk at easy pace; 70% of max HR

Example swim:

30–45 minute swim at aerobic pace; 70% of max HR

6. Easy Day (The Unofficial 6th)

The easy day is the often overlooked (and sometimes neglected) day that each exerciser needs. It is nearly impossible to go hard every day, and doing so can increase the risk of injury and/or burn-out. Sometimes recovery can be the missing piece to a good training program. Recovery days help the body prepare for harder days. A day off is necessary at times. Two to three days per week would be ideal for easy aerobic activity at a steady pace. These are the easiest training days of the week, but that doesn't mean that they are unimportant. Alternate activities can provide aerobic training benefits while allowing a specific muscle group to recover from the previous workouts. An example would be for a runner to swim on a cross-training day, or for a swimmer to cycle on a cross-training day.

Summary Questions

1. What are some health benefits to improved cardio-respiratory fitness?

2. Explain the FITT Principle. What are the ACSM Guidelines for FITT with moderate intensity exercise?

3. What are four common methods to assess intensity of cardiorespiratory activities?

4. What are the basic components of a cardiorespiratory exercise session?

5. Name and explain two of "The Big Six" types of training presented within Training Variations.

References

American College of Sports Medicine, Position Stand: quantity and quality of exercise for developing and maintaining cardiorespiratory, musculoskel-etal, and neuromotor fitness in apparently healthy adults: guidance for prescribing exercise. *Medicine & Science In Sports & Exercise*. 2011; 1334-1349.

American Council on Exercise. (2011). *ACE Integrated Fitness*. San Diego, CA: American Council on Exercise.

Brown, H.L. (1996). *Lifetime fitness*. Scottsdale, AZ: Gorsuch Scarisbrick, Publishers.

Corbin, C.B.; Lindsey, R.; Welk, G.J.; Corbin, W.B. (2002). *Concepts of fitness and wellness*. Boston: McGraw-Hill.

Daniels, J. (2005). *Daniel's Running Formula*. Champaign, IL: Human Kinetics.

Holly, R.G. & Shaffrath, J.D. (1998). Cardiorespira-tory endurance. In *ACSM's resource manual for guidelines for exercise testing and prescription* (pp. 437–447). Baltimore: Williams & Wilkins.

Howley, E.T. & Franks, B.D. (1997). *Health fitness instructor's handbook*. Champaign, IL: Human Ki-netics. McArdle, W.D.; Katch, F.I.; & Katch, V.L. (1996). *Exercise physiology*. Baltimore: Williams & Wilkins. Murray, T.D. & Murray, J.M. (1998). Cardiovascular anatomy. In *ACSM's resource man-ual for guidelines for exercise testing and prescription* (pp. 437-447). Baltimore: Williams & Wilkins.

Lydiard, A. & Gilmour, G. (2000). *Running with Lyd-iard*. Meyer & Meyer Sport.

Nieman, D.C. (1995). *Fitness and sports medicine: A health-related approach*. Mountain View, CA: May-field Publishing Company.

Prentice, W.E. (2001). *Get fit, stay fit*. Boston: Mc-Graw-Hill.

Web Sites

http://acsm.org/
American College of Sports Medicine

http://www.cooperaerobics.com
Cooper Aerobics Center

http://www.pe4life.org/
PE 4 Life

http://www.heart.org
American Heart Association

http://www.strokeassociation.org/
American Stroke Association

http://www.fitness.gov/
The President's Council on Physical Fitness & Sports

http://www.cdc.gov/physicalactivity
Center for Disease Control Physical Fitness Intensity Guidelines

http://www.verywell.com/rating-of-perceived-exertion-scale-3119445

http://www.runningforfitness.org

http://www.moxymonitor.com

Determining Your Target Heart Rate Zone for Exercise

Determining the appropriate target heart rate (THR) for exercise depends on an exerciser's resting heart rate, age, gender, and fitness level. The Karvonen Formula is preferred over the Maximum Heart Rate formula because it takes into account resting heart rate and gender. Rather than focus on a precise target heart rate (i.e., 140), a zone is calculated (i.e., 136–150). The purpose for achieving and staying within the THR zone is to maintain the appropriate intensity required for improvement of the cardiorespiratory system.

Here is the **Karvonen Formula** calculated for a **20-year-old male**, **Beginner Fitness Level**, with a **Resting Heart Rate of 68 beats per minute**. Use the chart to calculate your Target Heart Rate Zone.

Estimated Maximum Heart Rate (MHR): Men = 220 Women = 226[1]	MHR	220				MHR
	Age −	20				minus age
Predicted Maximum Heart Rate (PMHR) (Age Adjusted)	PMHR =	200				equals predicted maximum heart rate
	RHR −	68				minus resting heart rate
Resting Heart Rate (RHR) **Fitness Level:**	HRR =	132	132			equals heart rate reserve
Beginner 60–70% Intermediate 70–80%	Intensity ×	.60	.70	.80	.90	times intensity
Advanced 80–90%	=	79.2	92.4			equals
Target Heart Rate Zone: (in this example of a beginner	RHR +	68	68			plus resting heart rate
= 25–27 beats per 10 seconds)	=	147.2	160.4			equals
NOTE: For Swimming, MHR=205. This is due to: non-weight bearing activity, horizontal body position, and cooling effect of the water.	At 10 seconds ÷	6	6	6	6	60÷6=10 seconds
	Target Heart Rate =	24.5	26.7			beats per 10 seconds
[1] Women's hearts are smaller than men's and beat more times per minute.		60%	70%	80%	90%	

Use this chart to calculate your Target Heart Rate Zone.

Estimated Maximum Heart Rate (MHR): Men = 220 Women = 226[1]	MHR					MHR
	Age −					minus age
Predicted Maximum Heart Rate (PMHR)	PMHR =					equals predicted maximum heart rate
Resting Heart Rate (RHR)	RHR −					minus resting heart rate
Fitness Level:	HRR =					equals heart rate reserve
Beginner 60–70% Intermediate 70–80%	Intensity ×	.60	.70	.80	.90	times intensity
Advanced 80–90%	=					equals
Target Heart Rate Zone:	RHR +					plus resting heart rate
_____ to _____ beats per 10 seconds or	=					equals
_____ to _____ beats per 60 seconds	At 10 seconds ÷	6	6	6	6	60÷6=10 seconds
	Target Heart Rate =					beats per 10 seconds
[1] Women's hearts are smaller than men's and beat more times per minute.		60%	70%	80%	90%	

activity log

NAME		CLASS		DAY		HOUR	

DATE	TIME AM/PM	ACTIVITY	DURATION (MIN) and/or DISTANCE (LAPS/MILES)	CALORIES EXPENDED	HR/RPE	COMMENTS How Did You Feel? Tired, Sick, Good

DATE	TIME AM/PM	ACTIVITY	DURATION (MIN) and/or DISTANCE (LAPS/MILES)	CALORIES EXPENDED	HR/RPE	COMMENTS How Did You Feel? Tired, Sick, Good

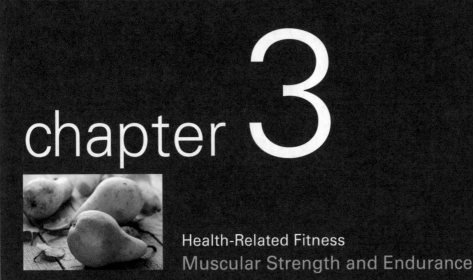

chapter 3

Health-Related Fitness
Muscular Strength and Endurance

by Darrin W. DeReu, MS, LAT, ATC

This chapter presents basic information regarding the development and maintenance of muscular fitness, muscular strength, and endurance. Although these three components of fitness can be developed using a variety of training methods or techniques, some form of weight training is probably the most efficient and popular method.

The benefits of weight training are discussed and important terms are defined. A simplified overview of the neuromuscular system and how it functions is presented. Basic guidelines are discussed, and finally, a description of weight lifting exercises and how to correctly perform them is provided.

A common question is "who will benefit from weight training?" Because all movement is the result of muscle contractions, it can be safely argued that most everyone will benefit. Stronger muscles are able to function more efficiently and will make all movements easier to perform. The more sedentary you are, the more likely it is that your level of strength and endurance is low, and hence you would benefit more than a very active individual. Although the level of strength that is appropriate will vary between individuals, depending upon the demands of their occupations and their leisure time pursuits, everyone should develop and maintain a healthy level of strength and muscular endurance throughout their life.

The Benefits of Weight Training

The benefits of weight training are widely recognized by the health and medical communities, and weight training has become one of the most often prescribed forms of exercise. Listed below are some of the potential benefits of weight training:

- Improvement or maintenance of strength and endurance

- An increase in power

- Improvement or maintenance of bone density

3

Chapter
Three

- An increase in the strength of connective tissue (tendons and ligaments)

- An increase and/or maintenance of lean mass— improved body composition

- Helps maintain resting metabolism as we age, which is directly linked to lean body mass

- Improvement or maintenance of flexibility

- Improved posture

- Enhanced self-image

- Provides a healthy outlet for stress

With regards to lean body tissue, the old adage "use it or lose it" is certainly applicable. Our bodies are very adaptable and will quickly lose their strength and endurance if not subjected to a regular form of overload. Because few people have occupations or engage in leisure time pursuits that are physically demanding, it is very important from a fitness standpoint to incorporate strength training into their total exercise program.

Common Terms in Weight Training

- **Strength**—the maximum force that can be generated by a muscle or group of muscles for a single repetition. Strength is dependent upon many factors, including muscle size, muscle attachments, fiber type, and motor unit recruitment.

- **Endurance**—the ability of a muscle to generate force for an extended period of time. Strength and endurance, although related, can be thought of as being at opposite ends of a continuum, with each requiring very specific training.

- **Power**—the ability to produce force rapidly. Work = force × distance and power = (force × distance) time. Power combines strength and speed, and is often the key factor in athletic success.

- **Flexibility**—the ability to move a joint through its full range of motion (ROM).

- **Repetition** (**rep**)—one complete movement of an exercise.

- **Set**—some number of repetitions performed consecutively. The number of repetitions in a set is determined by the goals of the trainee.

- **Atrophy**—a loss of body tissue that is associated with disuse. All lean body tissue is subject to atrophy.

- **Hypertrophy**—an increase in muscle mass associated with exercise. Hypertrophy is controlled to some degree by the hormone testosterone, so males generally see a greater amount of hypertrophy than females with the same level of training.

Types of Progressive Resistance Training

- **Isometrics**—a form of exercise that employs pulling and pushing against immovable objects where there is no visible lengthening or shortening of the muscles.

- **Isotonics**—a form of exercise characterized by exerting force against moveable objects such as barbells, dumbbells, and the use of various machines where the muscles go through both concentric and eccentric actions. Due to the lever system formed by the muscles, bones, and joints, the force generated will vary throughout the ROM. For example, with elbow flexion the biceps can produce maximal force when the elbow joint approaches 100 degrees but are relatively weaker at greater or lesser angles. For this reason, isotonics are subdivided into:

  - *Dynamic constant resistant exercises*—the use of free weights (i.e., barbells and dumbbells) where the resistance remains constant throughout the ROM.

  - *Dynamic variable resistance exercises*—the use of machines that employ a chain or belt that goes around an elliptically shaped cam that varies the resistance throughout the ROM. These machines are designed to match the resistance to the standard force curve for a given movement (i.e., the ability of the user to produce force).

- **Isokinetics**—a form of exercise machine that controls the speed of movement and provides a varying resistance throughout the ROM. The resistance the user encounters exactly mirrors the force produced at a constant speed. These machines are expensive and are not usually available to most individuals.

- **Plyometrics**—a form of exercise that involves the rapid eccentric loading of a muscle, which activates the stretch reflex, thereby recruiting more motor units. This form of training was originally developed to improve jumping ability and to bridge the gap between strength and speed training. An example is repetitive jumping on and off boxes.

Types of Muscle Actions

- **Isometric**—this type of muscle action occurs when the muscle shortens, exerting a force that is equal to the resistance and neither lengthens nor shortens.

- **Concentric**—this type of muscle action occurs when the muscle exerts a force that is greater than the resistance and shortens. For example, during the curl exercise, when the bar is curled from the straight arm position to the fully flexed position, the biceps are going through a concentric action.

- **Eccentric**—this type of muscle action occurs when the muscle exerts less force than the resistance and lengthens. Again, during the curl exercise, as the bar is lowered at a slow, controlled speed from the fully flexed position to the fully extended position, the biceps are going through an eccentric action. Weight trainers often refer to this type of training as negative reps. Interestingly, it has been determined that the delayed onset muscle soreness experienced after a workout is largely due to eccentric contractions.

Types of Weight Training

- **General Weight Training**—many people are recognizing the impact that training with weights can have on strength, endurance, and body composition. Most general weight training programs borrow from the following groups.

- **Olympic Weight Lifting**—a form of competitive weight lifting in which the athletes perform two lifts—the clean and jerk, and the snatch. This form of weight lifting requires great strength, power, athletic ability, and technique.

- **Power Lifting**—a form of competitive weight lifting in which the athletes perform three lifts—the bench press, the squat, and the dead-lift. This

form of lifting does not require the power and athletic ability of Olympic lifting. These three exercises develop many of the major muscle groups of the body and are used by both beginners and advanced weight trainers.

- **Body Building**—a form of competition where the participants are judged according to the size and symmetrical development of the entire musculature.

- **Sports Training**—almost all athletes use some form of weight training to improve strength, endurance, and power and to lessen the chances of injury. Identifying the demands of the sport enables trainers to develop specific exercise programs to meet these demands.

Training Principles

- **Overload**—This principle states that in order for positive adaptations to take place (improved strength, endurance, etc.) the body must be subjected to greater stress (exercise is a form of stress) than that to which it is accustomed. Productive overloading involves the proper use of its four components: load, repetition, rest, and frequency. The load or the intensity is the most important factor in strength development. Basically, strength is increased by lifting heavier weights and endurance is developed by performing more repetitions.

- **Specificity**—this principle states that how the body responds to exercise is dependent upon the type of stress and how the stress is applied. The adaptations that occur are very specific, so it is important to have goals and know how to train to reach these goals. The body builder and the Olympic weight lifter have different goals and therefore have very different training programs.

- **Reversibility**—often referred to as the "use it or lose it" principle, it states that any gains made through training will be lost with detraining. It has been determined, however, that the gains made can be maintained with less training than it took to achieve them.

- **Individual Differences**—this principle states that due to genetics, everyone's potential is different and progress will occur at different rates even when on identical training programs. Since few of us ever approach our genetic potential, we all can improve our fitness with proper training, good nutrition, and adequate rest.

The Anatomy and Physiology of Movement

All human motion is the result of muscle contractions, and with training, the functional capacity of these muscles can be greatly improved. In order for a muscle to contract, two things are required—energy in the form of adenosine triphosphate (ATP) and a stimulus from the central nervous system.

The arrangement of the bones of the skeletal system and how the muscles cross the various types of joints of the body determine the kinds of movement that are possible. For example, the elbow joint is a hinge joint that only allows for flexion and extension. The biceps and triceps cross the joint to the anterior and posterior respectively, and either flexion or extension will occur when they contract. A ball and socket joint like the hip is capable of many more movement patterns (flexion, extension, adduction, abduction, and circumduction). The muscles that cross this joint do so from many angles, and the movement that results from their contraction is the direct result of how they cross the joint.

Muscle contractions are very complex processes that are initiated from the central nervous system in the form of an electrical stimulus. Due to their structure and the interaction of various chemical processes, muscle tissue has the unique ability to contract. A cross-sectional view of a whole skeletal muscle reveals that it is composed of thousands of individual muscle cells or fibers. Within each fiber are smaller threadlike strands called myofibrils that contain the actual protein filaments (actin and myosin) that enable the muscle fibers to contract.

Movement occurs when the actin and myosin filaments slide past each other, shortening the fibers. All of the muscle fibers are grouped into bundles called fasciculi (muscle fiber bundles). Each individual fiber, fasciculi, and the entire muscle are all encased in layers of connective tissue.

These layers of connective tissue ultimately tie into the tendons that attach to the bones of the skeletal system. Acting as a harness, the force generated in the muscle is transmitted via this connective tissue/tendon to the bone, resulting in movement. The arrangement of the fasciculi determines a muscle's shape and is involved in its ability to generate force.

Each of the thousands of fibers in a muscle is stimulated by a nerve, a motor neuron. These motor neurons and the muscle fibers they activate are called motor units.

The force of a muscle contraction depends in large part on how many fibers are in a motor unit and how many motor units are recruited. This selective recruitment gives us the control necessary to produce movements requiring gradations of force, from the very delicate and accurate to the very powerful and gross.

Due to a natural level of inhibition we are unable, except perhaps in moments of extreme emotion, to recruit all the available motor units (a built-in safety feature). With training, however, we learn to recruit more motor units. Early strength gains experienced before muscle tissue has hypertrophied is mostly the result of the nervous system learning to recruit more motor units.

Muscle fibers (or more accurately motor units) are often classified according to their speed of contraction. Oversimplifying, the skeletal muscles' fibers can be classified as either fast twitch or slow twitch.

Although muscles typically have a mixture of slow and fast twitch fibers, all of the fibers in a motor unit are of the same type. For slow movements or movements that require little force, slow twitch fibers are recruited, and for faster movements or movements requiring more force, slow and fast twitch fibers are recruited.

Of special interest to the weight lifter is the fact that the body recruits muscle fibers in a set sequence, with slow fibers always the first to be recruited. Training with light resistance will not necessitate the recruitment and hence the development of fast twitch fibers. Due to their inherent qualities, fast twitch fibers have a greater capacity for anaerobic work (fast and intense) and slow twitch fibers have a greater capacity for aerobic work (endurance).

Research has shown that heredity largely determines the ratio of fast and slow twitch muscle fibers. With training, both slow and fast twitch fibers can take on some of the characteristics of the other fiber type, but conversion from one fiber type to the other does not seem to occur (at least not to any appreciable level).

Different Roles of Muscles

Skeletal muscles, which come in a wide variety of shapes, sizes, and fiber composition, are responsible for every movement. During a movement in which they are involved they can function in different roles. They can act as:

- **Agonists (prime movers)**—when they are primarily responsible for a movement.
  Example: the biceps' brachii during elbow flexion and during the curl

- **Antagonists**—when they produce the opposite action of the prime movers.
  Example: the triceps' brachii during elbow flexion and during the curl

- **Synergists**—when they assist the prime movers.
  Example: the brachioradialis during elbow flexion

- **Stabilizers**—when they help to stabilize the whole body or a particular body part.
  Example: the erector spinae stabilizes the spine during the curl

Movements

The human body is capable of an infinite variety of movements. The fundamental movements are listed and defined below. These movements are defined from a standardized starting position (standing erect with the feet parallel and close together, with the arms away from the body with the palms facing forward), referred to as the anatomical position. More complex movements are variations and combinations of these fundamental movements.

- **Flexion**—a movement that results in decreasing the joint angle. For example, in elbow flexion the angle between the forearm and the upper arm is decreased.

- **Extension**—a movement that results in increasing the joint angle. In elbow extension, the angle between the forearm and the upper arm is increased.

- **Adduction**—movement toward the midline of the body. Moving the arm toward the side as in the end of a jumping jack exercise involves shoulder adduction.

- **Abduction**—movement away from the midline of the body. Moving the arm away from the body during the start of a jumping jack involves shoulder abduction.

- **Rotation**—movement that occurs around the vertical axis of the body or around the long axis of a limb. Shaking your head "no" involves rotation of the head. With regard to movement of the limbs, rotation is described as either internal or external rotation. Moving the front surface of the arm or leg away from the midline of the body is defined as external rotation and moving the front surface toward the midline is defined as internal rotation.

- **Pronation**—rotating the forearm so that the palm faces either down or backward. You would use a pronated grip when doing the pull-up exercise or reverse curl.

- **Supination**—rotating the forearm so that the palm faces forward or up—you would use a supinated grip when performing a curl.

- **Plantar flexion**—at the ankle joint when the toes are moved away from the shin (pointing the toes). Performing the heel raise exercise involves plantar flexion when you go up on the balls of the foot.

- **Dorsi flexion**—at the ankle joint when the toes are moved toward the shin.

Weight Training Guidelines

Every workout should begin with a warm-up. A typical warm-up includes about five minutes of whole body cardio-type exercise to raise the heart rate, increase blood flow, and increase muscle temperature. This is followed by easy whole body stretching and then a specific warm-up of the muscles to be used (usually a light set). Each exercise should be done through a complete range of motion in a slow, controlled fashion. Make sure to control the exercise through both the concentric and eccentric phase of the exercise. It is usually recommended that you take 1 to 2 seconds to perform the concentric phase and 2 to 3 seconds to perform the eccentric phase. It is important to avoid holding your breath during the execution of an exercise. The general rule is to breathe in during the eccentric phase (typically when lowering the weight) and breathe out during the concentric phase (typically when raising the weight).

The first two to three weeks should be devoted to learning the correct technique and accustoming the body to the stress of lifting. Performing one set during the first week and gradually increasing the number of sets will aid in minimizing muscle soreness. Generally, allow 48 hours between weight training workouts for the same body part. A beginning program should consist of about 10 to 12 exercises that focus on the large muscle groups of the body. To ensure symmetrical development, include at least one exercise for each of the large muscle groups.

American College of Sports Medicine Guidelines

For general muscular fitness, the American College of Sports Medicine recommends 1–3 sets of 8–12 repetitions 2–3 times a week. You should select multi-joint exercises that require the requirement of multi-muscle groups (bench press, overhead press, rowing exercises, squats, leg presses, etc.). Isolation exercises that involve a single joint and focus on less muscle mass should be used to complement your program.

The program should be progressive and repeat itself periodically. Accomplish this by increasing the resistance in a systematic and regular fashion and by repeating the exercises on a regular basis (Monday, Wednesday, Friday, for example). Incorporate variability into your program with respect to the exercises performed and the intensity at which they are performed. Learn a number of exercises for each large muscle group, and on different days, work at a different level of intensity.

The FITT principle frequency (intensity, time, and type of training), give shape to your program and will largely determine the level of improvement and success. The adaptations and improvement experienced will be specific to the frequency, intensity, and volume of training—remember, training for general health and fitness requires much less effort than training for maximal sports performance.

Selecting the amount of weight to use in training will be determined by your goals and is usually based on a percent of your 1 Rep Max (RM): the maximum weight that you can lift through a full ROM one time. Most research indicates that a load equal to about 75% of 1 RM is necessary to promote strength gains. Most people can perform about 10 reps using 75% of their 1 RM.

Do not attempt a 1 RM until you have mastered the lift and have been engaged in strength training for 4 to 6 weeks. The 1 RM can be approximated by using the Brown formula: Maximum Weight = [(Reps × .0328) + .9849] × Resistance.

The following chart will help in determining the resistance and the number of sets and reps to use in training for different goals:

TRAINING GOAL	RESISTANCE	NUMBER OF REPS	NUMBER OF SETS
Strength/power	Heavy	2 to 6	2 to 3
Endurance	Light	15 to 25	2 to 3
General conditioning	Medium	8 to 12	1 to 3

The amount of rest between sets is determined by your training goals, the system of training you are using, and how much weight you are lifting. Training for strength and using a 2 to 6 RM/set in a priority system will require 2 to 3 minutes rest between sets. Super-setting will allow you to decrease this rest time.

Always perform the exercises that involve large muscle groups and are multi-joint type exercises first (bench press, overhead press, rowing exercises, squats, leg presses, etc.). If single joint or small muscle group exercises are performed first, these small muscles will become the limiting factor rather than the large muscle groups you are trying to exercise. For instance, performing curls prior to pull-ups will pre-fatigue the biceps and make it difficult to adequately work the large, stronger muscles of the back.

There are several systems for determining the number of sets, repetitions, resistance, and order of exercises. The following outlines a few of the more common systems.

- **Circuit Training**—a system of training where the individual performs a single set of a number of different exercises with a minimum amount of rest in between. The circuit can then be repeated until the desired number of sets for each exercise is met. This system is time efficient and is effective in developing muscular endurance and general conditioning and in maintaining a certain degree of fitness.

EXERCISE	WEIGHT	REPS
Shoulder Press	Medium	10
Bent-Over Rows	Medium	10
Standing Dumbbell Curls	Medium	10
Tricep Dips	Body weight	15
Push Ups	Body weight	15
90 Seconds Rest, Repeat as many times as desired		

- **Pyramid**—a system of training where an individual performs a single exercise for 3 or more sets, increasing the resistance with each set. This system may also be reversed for a *Descending Pyramid System*. This system can help to overcome a lifting plateau and produce good muscular strength gains.

Exercise: Bench Press

SET	WEIGHT	REPS
1	Light	12–16
2	Light/Medium	10–12
3	Medium	8–10
4	Heavy	4–6

- **Super Set**—a system that utilizes two exercises, generally with opposing muscle groups, in rapid succession with a short break in between. For example, a chest exercise is performed immediately followed by a back exercise then a short rest period before repeating that process. Super-setting is very popular when workout time is a factor as it allows for several exercises to be performed quickly.

EXERCISES	WEIGHT	REPS
Bench Press	Light, Medium or Heavy	12–16, 8–10, 4–6
Lat Pull Down	Light, Medium or Heavy	12–16, 8–10, 4–6
60 Seconds of Rest, Repeat as many times as desired		

- **Giant Set**—a system that utilizes multiple exercises in succession for the same muscle group. This type of system is often done to failure with a reduction of weight halfway through as the muscle group fatigues. Giant-setting should be utilized sparingly as it can cause significant fatigue and possible

delayed onset muscle soreness. However, it can be effective in overcoming a lifting plateau and does produce significant muscular strength gains.

EXERCISE	WEIGHT	REPS
Dumbbell Bench Press	Medium	8–12
Cable Dumbbell Fly	Medium	8–12
Barbell Incline Bench Press	Medium	8–12
Wide Grip Push Up	Body Weight	8–12

- **Drop Set**—a system in which an individual performs as many repetitions as possible then immediately drops the weight 10–15% and again performs as many repetitions as possible. This process can be repeated to complete failure. Similar to giant-setting, this system should generally be used sparingly as it pushes muscles to their absolute maximum capacity, which may cause significant fatigue and soreness.

Exercise: Bicep Curl

SET	WEIGHT	REP
1	40 lb	To fatigue
2	30 lb	To fatigue
3	20 lb	To fatigue
4	10 lb	To fatigue

Safety

Safety is important at all times when lifting. The purpose of any physical training is to improve upon your present condition. Injuries due to poor form or lifting techniques can slow or stop your progress. The correct technique should be used to perform each exercise through the proper range of motion in a controlled fashion. Correct technique includes maintaining proper body positioning and alignment, breathing, and moving the joint through its full range of motion utilizing only the muscles that are appropriate.

The spine is very strong when the normal curves are maintained in what is called neutral spine, and therefore to protect the spine, lifts should be completed with a neutral spine. Spinal rotation and rounding the lower back during the execution of most exercises should be avoided.

It is important to breathe through each repetition and therefore it is important to avoid holding your breath during the lift. A spotter, someone to assist if the lift cannot be completed, should be used when lifting weights above the body. Collars or clips should be used to keep the weight plates on the bar. Sliding plates can unbalance the bar and result in injury. Weight rooms are often busy and crowded. Be aware of what is going on around you and be prepared to protect your safety. Keeping a record of your training program that includes details of the weight, the number of sets and reps, and a brief descriptive analysis of the training session can be very valuable. To get the full benefits of weight training, progressive overload is necessary, and by maintaining a record it is easy to ensure appropriate weight increases occur.

In addition to ensuring progressive overload, record-keeping can be a motivational tool. It is important to realize that due to the principle of individual differences, everyone will progress at different rates even when on the same program. Your progress and success are going to be largely determined by the consistency and intensity of your training. Therefore, it is important to set realistic goals that result in the symmetrical development of all the major muscle groups of the body.

Basic Weight Training Exercises

Although there are virtually hundreds of different weight lifting exercises, most are variations of a relative few. For instance, the bench press can be performed on a flat bench, incline bench, decline bench, with barbells or dumbbells, or using a machine. Listed below are some of the basic lifts that should be incorporated into most programs.

■ Bench Press

Prime Movers: pectorals, anterior deltoid, triceps

Execution: Lie in a supine position on the bench with the feet flat on the floor. Grasp the bar with a pronated grip (palm away) and the hands a little wider than shoulder width. Slowly lower the bar until it touches the chest at the nipple line and then push the bar back to starting position. Do not bounce the bar off the chest or arch the back during the exercise.

■ Overhead Press

Prime Movers: deltoid, trapezius

Execution: The overhead press shown is being performed on a specialized overhead press machine. The seat should be adjusted so the exercise is started with the hands just above shoulder height. The arms are then pressed overhead until the elbows are fully extended and returned to the starting position. Most machines will offer multiple hand positions. The back should be kept in a neutral position and rested against the seat back.

■ Lat Pulldown

Prime Movers: latissimus dorsi, teres major, rhomboids, biceps

Execution: Use a grip slightly wider than shoulder width with the palms facing away. Pull the bar down either in front of or behind your head to shoulder height. Keep your body in an erect position and avoid leaning back at the waist during the exercise. Using a narrow grip puts more emphasis on the biceps.

■ Seated Row

Prime Movers: rhomboids, latissimus dorsi

Execution: The Seated Row shown is performed on a specialized Seated Row Machine. Grasp the handles of the machine (many machines will offer several handle options). Sit down with the spine in a neutral position and knees slightly bent. Pull the arms straight back, keeping the elbows near the rib cage, then return to the starting position.

■ Upright Row

Prime Movers: trapezius, deltoids

Execution: this exercise is performed in a standing position with the feet about shoulder width apart. The barbell is held against the front of the thighs with the arms fully extended, using a pronated grip. Keeping the bar close to the body, pull it up to the height of the clavicle. Avoid leaning forward to initiate the movement or backward to complete the movement.

■ Squats

Prime Movers: gluteus maximus, quadriceps, hamstrings

Execution: Squats are a multi-joint whole body exercise that works many stabilizing muscles in addition to the prime movers. They are one of the best overall exercises when done correctly. All beginners are recommended to have an instructor or experienced weight lifter assist them in learning the correct technique when first attempting this lift. With the barbell on the shoulders, stand with the feet about shoulder width apart, toes angled slightly outward. Slowly squat until the top of the thighs are parallel with the floor. Try not to let your knees go out over your toes. Keep your head up, eyes looking straight ahead or upward, your torso nearly vertical, and your back slightly arched. Do not round your back or allow the head to drop, as this will put tremendous stress upon your lower back. Maintain good body position, and without bouncing at the bottom, return to the starting position. Throughout the exercise, keep your feet flat on the floor—don't go up on the balls of the feet.

■ Leg Press

Prime Movers: gluteus maximus, quadriceps, hamstrings

Execution: This exercise is performed on a leg press machine. Place your feet on the platform about shoulder width apart with your toes angled slightly outward. Lower the weight until the knees are at about a ninety-degree angle. Without bouncing at the bottom, push the weight back up to the starting position. Although the legs will be straight at the completion of the movement, avoid locking the knees.

■ Leg Curl

Prime Movers: hamstrings

Execution: This exercise is normally performed on a special leg curl machine. Begin the exercise in a prone position with the padded bar across the back of your legs just above the ankles. Curl the moveable pad toward your buttocks by flexing your knees until it contacts the back of your legs. Slowly return to the starting position.

■ Leg Extension

Prime Movers: quadriceps

Execution: This exercise is normally performed on a special leg extension machine. Adjust the machine so that the leading edge of the seat touches the back of your knees when you are sitting with your legs hanging straight down. The padded bar should be just above your ankles. Extend your knees until the legs are straight and then hold this position momentarily. Because of potential stresses in the knee joint, only lower the weight about 30 degrees. This is especially true if you are lifting heavy weights.

■ Heel Raises

Prime Movers: gastrocnemius, soleus

Execution: This exercise is usually done on a special machine but can be performed with a barbell or dumbbells. If you are in a standing (or straight-leg) position, both the gastrocnemius and the soleus are involved in the exercise. If you are in a seated (or bent-knee) position, only the soleus is involved—so the seated form of this exercise will seem harder. Keeping your legs extended (all movement should occur at the ankle joint), forcefully raise your heels as high as possible and then lower to the starting position.

■ Back Extensions

Prime Movers: erector spinae, gluteus maximus

Execution: This exercise can be most effectively and comfortably performed on a special apparatus. Start with your torso extending beyond the edge of the apparatus at 90 degrees with your lower body. Extend your trunk until your back is parallel with the floor—do not hyperextend—and then slowly return to the starting position.

■ Curls

Prime Movers: biceps brachii, brachialis, brachioradialis

Execution: Stand erect with your feet about shoulder width apart and grasp the bar with a supinated grip. Your hands should be about shoulder width apart and your arms fully extended, so that the bar touches the front of your thighs. Keep your elbows stationary as the bar is curled (bar moves in an arc toward your shoulders) until your arms are fully flexed. Lower the bar to the starting position. Avoid leaning forward or backward to help curl the weight.

■ Tricep Extension

Prime Movers: triceps

Execution: This exercise is performed on a cable resistance machine. The example shown is utilizing the V-Bar handle but there are other possible handles, such as the rope and straight bar. Begin with the elbows flexed so the hands are positioned anterior to the shoulders with the elbows near the rib cage. Extend the elbows pushing the hands just anterior to the hips and then return to the starting position. The upper arm should remain stationary throughout this exercise.

■ Abdominal Exercises

Prime Movers: rectus abdominus

The muscles in the abdomen perform a number of important functions. They flex and assist in rotating the trunk and support and contain the abdominal organs. Weak abdominal muscles have been identified as a contributing cause of lower back pain. There are several exercises that address the abdominal muscles.

Execution: The examples shown are variations of the abdominal crunch. The arms can be placed across the chest or at the sides, depending on desired difficulty. The upper torso should be raised so the shoulder blades are completely off the ground keeping the lower back in contact with the ground. Care should be taken to keep the neck in a neutral position to avoid straining the neck, especially if there is a history of neck problems.

■ Regular Push-Ups

Prime Movers: pectoralis major

Execution: The push-up is performed by facing the ground with arms extended and body in a straight line. The hands should be placed just wider than shoulder width apart on the ground. The body is then lowered down until the elbow reaches approximately 90 degrees of flexion maintaining the body in a straight line. Then return to the starting position.

■ Modified Push-Ups

Prime Movers: pectoralis major

Execution: If less resistance is desired then a modified push-up can be utilized by placing the knees on the ground and performing the same movement.

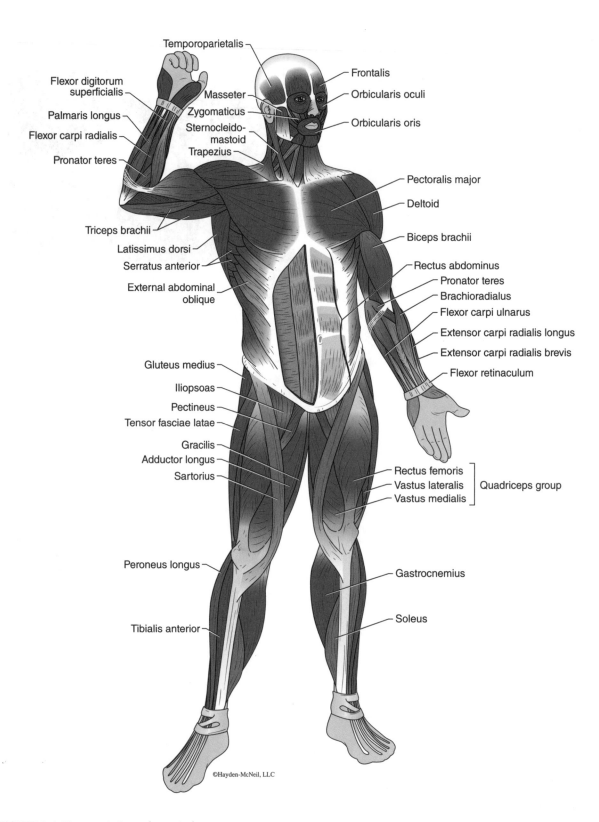

FIGURE 3-1. Human skeleton (anterior).

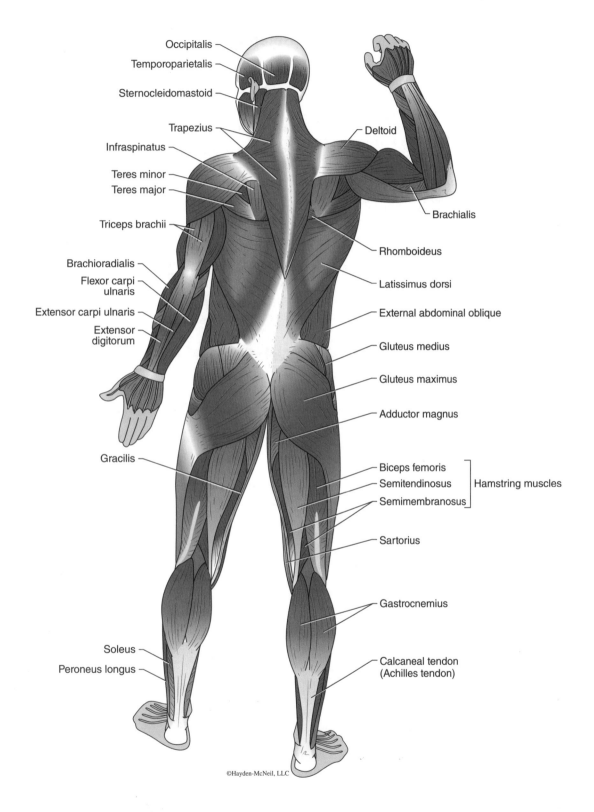

©Hayden-McNeil, LLC

FIGURE 3-2. Human skeleton (posterior).

Summary Questions

1. Who can benefit from weight training?

2. What are the benefits of weight training?

3. What are the four principles of weight training?

4. What are the four types of progressive resistance training?

5. How does resistance, number of repetitions and number of sets change according to your training goals?

References

American College of Sports Medicine (2006). *ACSM's Guidelines for Exercise Testing and Prescription* (6th edition). Philadelphia: Lipincott/Williams & Wilkins.

Baechle, T. & Earle, R. (2001). *Essentials of Strength Training and Conditioning* (2nd edition). Champaign, II: Human Kinetics.

Behnke, R. (2001). *Kinetic Anatomy* Champaign, II: Human Kinetics.

Hesson, J. (2003). *Weight Training for Life* (6th edition). Wadsworth/Thomson.

Moran, G. & McGlynn (2001). *Dynamics of Strength Training and Conditioning* (3rd edition). New York: McGraw-Hill.

Web Sites

http://www.acsm.org
American College of Sports Medicine

http://www.nsca.com
National Strength and Conditioning Association

http://www.nata.org
National Athletic Training Association

weight training log

NAME		CLASS		DAY		HOUR	

	DATE							

Exercises	Sets	Weight	Reps	Weight	Reps	Weight	Reps	Weight	Reps	Weight	Reps	Weight	Reps
	1												
	2												
	3												
	1												
	2												
	3												
	1												
	2												
	3												
	1												
	2												
	3												
	1												
	2												
	3												
	1												
	2												
	3												
	1												
	2												
	3												
	1												
	2												
	3												
	1												
	2												
	3												
	1												
	2												
	3												

Exercises	Sets	Weight	Reps	Weight	Reps	Weight	Reps	Weight	Reps	Weight	Reps	Weight	Reps
DATE													
	1												
	2												
	3												
	1												
	2												
	3												
	1												
	2												
	3												
	1												
	2												
	3												
	1												
	2												
	3												
	1												
	2												
	3												
	1												
	2												
	3												
	1												
	2												
	3												
	1												
	2												
	3												
	1												
	2												
	3												
	1												
	2												
	3												
	1												
	2												
	3												

chapter 4

Health-Related Fitness
Flexibility

by Marsha Lester, MS; Beth Fath, M.F.A.

Flexibility Guidelines

Flexibility is defined as the ability to move a joint through its full range of motion (ROM). Stretching, the means by which we increase flexibility, is used to prepare muscles for the upcoming workout, enhance performance, and aid in returning the body to its pre-exercise state.

<u>Benefits of Increasing and Maintaining Flexibility</u>

- Increased production and retention of lubricants between connective tissue

- Reduction in the severity and frequency of muscular injuries

- Slows down the loss of joint mobility associated with aging

- Aids in developing and maintaining proper posture, thus reducing potential back pain

- Increased performance in specific athletic activities

- May prevent, delay, and/or lessen pain associated with arthritis

- Improvement in balance, stability, and coordination in the elderly

- Reduction in stiffness, tightness, and muscular tension

- Better neuromuscular coordination

4

___

Chapter
Four

Four Methods of Stretching

- **Ballistic**

  This form of stretching is characterized by the use of speed and force to produce rapid, repetitive bouncing or jerking movements. Uncontrolled movements via this type of stretching can cause soreness or injury and is not widely recommended. The American Academy of Orthopaedic Surgeons (AAOS) and most experts warn against ballistic stretching. This type of stretching may be too forceful and can cause damage to joint soft tissue (i.e., ligaments).

- **Dynamic**

  This type of stretching is considered a safe form of the ballistic method. It incorporates gradual and controlled movements to bring muscles through a full range of motion around a joint. The movements imitate the upcoming sport or physical activity in a less intense manner and are widely used during the warm-up phase. This form of stretching is more widely recommended than ballistic stretching.

- **Static**

  These stretches are performed by slowly moving into an extended position, holding the position for a period of time, and then returning to a resting length. There is little pain and a low risk for injury. This form of stretching is normally used during the cool-down and is a highly recommended method for effectively developing flexibility.

- **Proprioceptive Neuromuscular Facilitation (PNF)**

  This type of stretching consists of alternating an isometric muscular contraction followed by passive stretching. There are various techniques that may be applied when performing this type of stretching, with the most popular being a "contract-relax-contract" method. This method consists of stretching the target muscle, isometrically contracting the muscle for several seconds, then relaxing the muscle and immediately stretching the muscle using gravity or assistance. PNF stretching can be the most effective method of increasing flexibility, but it is time-consuming and usually requires assistance.

As with the other components of fitness, we can use the acronym FITT to follow in developing and maintaining flexibility.

F requency	2–3 days per week (ideal is 5–7 per week)
I ntensity	stretch to mild discomfort
T ime	hold for 15–30 seconds/2–4 reps
T ype	static, dynamic, PNF

Exercise Warm-Up Guidelines

Cardiorespiratory

The warm-up phase gradually prepares the individual's body for exercise. All activities/workouts need a warm-up phase and it needs to be done first. The warm-up should heat up and loosen the body. A proper warm-up should have all joints moving and then progress through movements that will loosen and stretch the muscle groups. It takes the body from a resting state into one of moderate to vigorous activity. Increased muscle temperature, a greater range of motion, enhanced performance, and injury prevention are the primary outcomes desired from the warm-up. Execution of the warm-up should take into consideration the individual's age, physical limitations, capabilities, environmental conditions, and the requirements of the upcoming activity or workout.

The cardiorespiratory warm-up should be at least five minutes in length. The speed of movement gradually increases from a slow to moderate pace and the movement around the joints being used should gradually increase. All movement should be smooth and rhythmic. Typically the warm-up includes low-intensity movements that are similar to the upcoming activity or workout.

Stretching

Stretching does not replace the warm-up phase but is part of it. The focus of stretching is on major muscle groups and is specific to the sport or activity. Recent research studies question the effects and benefits of stretching as a part of the warm-up phase. Research is showing that activities that require explosive power, strength, or jumping may see a decrease in performance with pre-activity static stretching. The studies show if static stretch is held for more than 60 seconds, there may be a brief inability to generate power. Short static stretch (15–30 seconds) has a better outcome and, when added to the warm-up phase, there is a lower risk of muscle strain or tear. Most experts agree it is best to do more dynamic stretching.

Not all activities need pre-exercise stretching. For example, runners and cyclists have a low risk of acute muscle strain. Therefore, stretching before these activities offer little protection against acute injury. Runners and cyclists can adequately warm up with light/slow jogging or pedaling.

For general fitness activities and selected sports, low intensity static stretching may be utilized during the warm-up once the body's core temperature has increased from its resting level (core temperature will rise about half a degree for every five minutes of warm-up). These stretches are performed until mild discomfort is felt and held for 15–30 seconds. Each stretch should be executed in a relaxed, controlled manner. Stretching that results in hyperextension, hyperflexion, or extreme rotation should be avoided. Continued research is needed to clarify the benefits of stretching on performance and its impact related to injury.

Exercise Cool-Down Guidelines

Cardiorespiratory

The cool-down phase of exercise is just as important as the warm-up phase. This part of the workout returns the body to its pre-activity resting state. The individual begins with an easy cardiorespiratory phase that allows the heart rate to drop, followed by stretching muscle groups used in the specific workout or activity. A cardiorespiratory cool-down should always be the first part of the total cool-down phase. This is typically a very low intensity version of the exercise routine. For example, if you run for your activity, you will probably choose to cool down with a jog and/or a walk. This gradual decrease in intensity allows the heart to adjust properly. It should be about 3–5 minutes in length, long enough for the heartbeat to return to baseline range and breathing to return to normal.

Stretching

Stretching should always follow the cardiorespiratory cool-down once the heart rate and breathing have returned to pre-activity levels. Stretching should be done long enough to adequately stretch all the major muscle groups used in the activity. Static stretching is the most commonly used and preferred method during post-activity. Each stretch should be held 15–30 seconds with 1–4 repetitions performed for each muscle. All stretches should be performed slowly in a relaxed and controlled manner. It is important to never force a stretch and to spend equal time on each side of the body. Always maintain continuous breathing throughout the stretches and avoid holding the breath at any time.

Stretching after the activity/workout reduces injury as well as muscle soreness. An added benefit of stretching is increased flexibility. This is best accomplished when performed at the end of a workout or activity. At this time the muscles are warm and supple because blood circulation has increased, therefore the muscles are able to attain a maximum stretch. To maintain or improve flexibility, stretching should be completed a minimum of two times a week.

If time permits, a final phase of relaxation techniques can be incorporated into the cool down to aid in the total release of tension for the individual. These techniques consist of slow deep breathing exercises and combinations of isometric muscle contractions, followed by relaxing individual muscle groups. Better flexibility results in better fitness.

EFFECTS OF WARM-UP	EFFECTS OF COOL-DOWN
• Increased heart rate • Increased blood flow, stroke volume, and oxygen exchange • Increased muscle and blood temperature • Increased speed and strength of muscle contractions • Decreased muscle soreness, muscle/tendon strains, and muscle/tendon tears • Increased range of motion • Increased muscle, tendon, and ligament elasticity • Decreased muscle tension • Increased psychological preparedness	• Aids in circulatory and metabolic exercise rates returning to normal levels • Decreases muscle cramps • Decreases muscle fatigue • Increases tendon, ligament, and muscle elasticity • Decreases post-exercise muscle soreness • Decreases muscle stiffness • Decreases risk of dizziness and fainting • Prevents a pooling of blood in the veins • Aids in dispersement of lactic acid • Promotes relaxation of the mind and body • Decreases body temperature

Assessing Flexibility

There is no one test that can test the overall flexibility of an individual. Remember, the definition of flexibility is the ability to move a joint through its full range of motion. Therefore, each joint may have different levels of flexibility with different tests required to gain that measure. A common test that is used to assess lower back and hamstring flexibility is called the sit-and-reach test. This test is performed by sitting against a solid wall with the legs extended in front and the feet resting flat against a box. Sitting tall against the wall, arms should be extended with middle fingers stacked. The individual being tested will slide his/her fingers across the top of the ruler three separate times with the best score taken.

Flexibility

Flexibility will be tested by a modified sit-and-reach test. Shoes should be removed. You will sit on the floor with your back against the wall, legs extended in front of you with your feet flat against the measurement box. A ruler is placed on top of the box so that it extends 15″ over the end of the box, with the zero mark toward you. Make sure your hips are pulled back against the wall. With your shoulder blades against the wall, extend your arms out in front and slide your hands (hand over hand) along the ruler as far as you can without bending at the knees. This will be completed 3 times and the highest score will be recorded. The grading scale is to the right.

FLEXIBILITY 10 points			
Grade	Scale Score	Raw Score	
		Male	Female
A	10	23+	24+
	9.9	22.5	23.5
	9.8	22	23
	9.6	22.5	22.5
	9.4	21	22
	9.2	20.5	21.5
	9	20	21
B	8.9	19.5	20.5
	8.8	19	20
	8.6	18.5	19.5
	8.4	18	19
	8.2	17.5	18.5
	8	17	18
C	7.9	16.5	17.5
	7.8	16	17
	7.6	15.5	16.5
	7.4	15	16
	7.2	14.5	15.5
	7	14	15
D	6.9	13.5	14.5
	6.8	13	14
	6.6	12.5	13.5
	6.4	12	13
	6.2	11.5	12.5
	6	11	12
F	5.9	10.5	11.5
	5.8	10	11
	5.6	9.5	10.5
	5.4	9	10

Source: Cooper Institute (2008). Physical Fitness Standards, pgs. 28–35.

Stretching Exercises

The following stretches are common stretches that can be used for both the warm-up and cool-down phase of your exercise program. They focus on the major muscle groups in the body used for many activities. Choose the type of stretches (Static, Dynamic or PNF) that will enhance your exercise program, but remember to never stretch to a point of discomfort.

■ Lateral Head Tilt

FIGURE 4-1. Head tilt.   **FIGURE 4-2.** Head tilt.

a. Purpose: To stretch your neck flexors and extensors, and ligaments of the cervical spine.

b. Starting position: Keep your head upright with your neck perpendicular to the floor.

c. Movement (Figures 4-1 and 4-2): Slowly and gently tilt your head laterally and drop your opposite shoulder gently to increase the stretch as shown in Figure 4-1. Hold for 15 to 30 seconds. Return your head to the upright position before stretching to the opposite side. To stretch the back of your neck you may gently drop your chin as shown in Figure 4-2.

d. Precaution: Damage to the cervical discs may occur if you roll your neck in circles instead of bringing your head to the upright position before stretching in another direction.

■ Shoulder Stretches

Stretch 1

a. Purpose: To stretch your shoulders, chest and upper back.

b. Starting position (Figure 4-3): Place your left arm across your chest with your right forearm supporting your left arm.

c. Movement: With your right forearm, pull your left arm gently toward your right shoulder and hold for 15 to 30 seconds as shown in Figure 4-3. Switch arms and repeat stretch to stretch opposite shoulder. Make sure that you keep your shoulder down and away from your ear during the stretch. In Figure 4-3 the person on your left has her shoulder down (correct); the person on your right is incorrect.

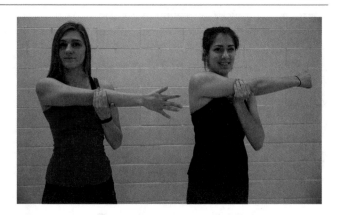

FIGURE 4-3. Shoulder stretch 1.

Stretch 2

a. Purpose: To stretch the shoulders, chest and upper back.

b. Starting position (Figure 4-4): Extend your left hand over your left shoulder and reach your right hand up the middle of your back to grasp your left hand as shown on the right. You may use a towel, band or belt to extend your reach if you can't clasp your hands together as shown on the left.

c. Movement: Pull downward gently with your lower hand. Breathe in as you stretch downward, holding the stretch for 15 to 30 seconds. Switch arms and hands to stretch your other shoulder. Maintain neutral torso alignment during the stretch. Do not drop the head or allow the ribs or pelvis to protrude as is shown in Figure 4-5.

FIGURE 4-4. Shoulder stretch 2.

FIGURE 4-5. Shoulder stretch 2.

■ **Chest and Shoulder Stretch**

a. Purpose: To stretch the chest and front of the shoulders.

b. Starting position (Figure 4-6): Stand perpendicular to a wall with your left hand on the wall (palm facing the wall) at shoulder height as shown in Figure 4-6.

c. Movement: Gently turn your body away from the wall and your hand to increase the stretch. Hold the stretch for 15 to 30 seconds. Repeat the stretch with the other arm while facing the opposite direction to stretch your other shoulder. Do not allow the elbow to hyperextend. If that is your tendency, maintain a small bend in the elbow of the arm on the wall.

FIGURE 4-6. Chest and shoulder stretch.

■ **Side Stretch**

a. Purpose: To stretch your torso.

b. Starting position (Figure 4-7): Start with your legs crossed and your right arm extended upward, in line with your shoulder. Place your left hand on the ground off of your left hip for support. Lean over slightly toward your left hand (that is on the ground) as shown in Figure 4-7.

c. Movement (Figure 4-8): Twist your stomach so that you look up toward the sky as shown in Figure 4-8. Be sure to keep both sit bones on the ground and hold the stretch for 15 to 30 seconds. Switch arms and lean to the opposite side to stretch the opposite side of your torso.

FIGURE 4-7. Side stretch.   **FIGURE 4-8.** Side stretch.

■ Back Stretch

Stretch 1

a.   Purpose: To stretch your upper and lower back muscles.

b.   Starting position (Figures 4-9 and 4-10): Soften your knees by bending them slightly, round your spine and keep your head down. Let your hands hang loosely and relaxed by keeping them "heavy" as shown in Figure 4-9. A modification of the starting position is to place your hands slightly above your knees so they are supported as shown in Figure 4-10.

c.   Movement: Gently arch your back and lower your shoulders to increase the stretch in your back. Hold the stretch for 15–30 seconds.

 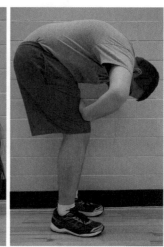

FIGURE 4-9. Back stretch.   **FIGURE 4-10.** Back stretch.

Stretch 2

a.   Purpose: To dynamically stretch back muscles.

b.   Starting position (Figures 4-11 and 4-12): Start on hands and knees. Keep the shoulders aligned with hands and pelvis aligned with knees.

c.   Movement: Round your spine upward and let your head and tailbone be heavy as shown in Figure 4-11. Gently reverse the curve of the spine, looking forward as you pull the chest forward and the pelvis back as shown in Figure 4-12. Keep moving back and forth, coordinating with your breath.

FIGURE 4-11. Back stretch 2.

FIGURE 4-12. Back stretch 2.

Stretch 3

a. Purpose: To stretch back muscles.

b. Starting position (Figure 4-13): Lie/lay on your back with your pelvis off to the right side and your knees to your chest. Have your arms out to the side with your palms facing up.

c. Movement: Roll onto the left side of your pelvis and rest the legs on the floor. Hold the stretch for 15-30 seconds. Engage your abs as you roll back onto your back, then bring your feet to the floor. Move the pelvis off to the left and reverse the stretch.

FIGURE 4-13. Back stretch 3.

■ Hip Flexor and Lower Leg

Stretch 1

a. Purpose: To stretch your hip flexor and calf.

b. Starting position (Figures 4-14 and 4-15): Face the wall and place both hands flat against the wall while your feet are staggered. Slightly bend your front leg; the heels of both feet should be placed flat on the floor as shown in Figure 4-14.

c. Movement: While keeping your body straight, sink your hips forward and weight your rear heel to stretch both your hip flexor and calf. Hold the stretch for 15 to 30 seconds. Keeping the back heel on the floor, bend the back knee a little, stretching the front of the lower leg as shown in Figure 4-15. Hold the stretch for 15–30 seconds. Switch the position of your legs to stretch your other hip flexor and calf.

FIGURE 4-14. Hip flexor and lower leg stretch 1.   **FIGURE 4-15.** Hip flexor and lower leg stretch 1.

Stretch 2

   a.   Purpose: To stretch your hip flexor as shown in Figure 4-17.

   b.   Starting position (Figures 4-16 and 4-17): Start with your left foot forward and make sure your shin is perpendicular to the floor (or your left knee is over your left foot). Extend your right leg behind you and drop your right knee on the floor with the top of your right foot on the floor as shown in Figure 4-16.

   c.   Movement: Drop hips forward toward your front foot to stretch your hip flexor as shown in Figure 4-17. Hold the stretch for 15 to 30 seconds. Switch legs to stretch your opposite hip flexor.

FIGURE 4-16. Hip flexor and lower leg stretch 2.

FIGURE 4-17. Hip flexor and lower leg stretch 2.

■ **Hamstring Stretch**

Stretch 1

    a.   Purpose: To stretch the back of the thigh (hamstrings).

    b.   Starting position (Figure 4-18): Stand on your left leg with your left knee bent. Put your right heel in front of you with a straight knee as shown in Figure 4-18.

    c.   Movement: Keep your back straight and fold forward at the hip joint to feel stretch in back of leg. Hold the stretch for 15 to 30 seconds. Switch the position of your legs to stretch your other hamstring.

FIGURE 4-18.
Hamstring stretch 1.

Stretch 2

    a.   Purpose: To stretch the back of the thigh (hamstrings).

    b.   Starting position (Figure 4-19): Lie on your back and loop a strap over the arch of your foot out on the diagonal. Have your other leg extended on the floor.

    c.   Movement: Using the strap bring your leg up until you feel a mild to moderate stretch in the back of the leg as shown in Figure 4-19. The floor leg should be gently pressing down into the floor. Hold the stretch for 15 to 30 seconds. Bend the knee to remove the strap. Loop the strap over the other leg and reverse the stretch.

FIGURE 4-19.
Hamstring stretch 2.

■ Hip Extensor Stretch

a. Purpose: To stretch the hip extensors (buttocks).

b. Starting position (Figure 4-20): Lay flat on the floor with chest facing upward, arms to the side and your right leg bent. Place your left foot in front of your right knee so your left shin is parallel to the floor. Your legs in this position should resemble the number four as shown in Figure 4-20.

c. Movement (Figure 4-21): Place both hands on the back of your right leg (hamstring) and gently pull your right leg toward your chest as shown in Figure 4-21. You should feel the stretch in your hip extensors (buttocks). Hold the stretch for 15 to 30 seconds. Switch the position of your legs to stretch the opposite side.

FIGURE 4-20. Hip extensor stretch.

FIGURE 4-21. Hip extensor stretch.

■ Inner Thigh, Groin and Buttocks (Gluteus Maximus) Stretch

a. Purpose: To stretch inner thigh, groin and buttocks area.

b. Starting position (Figure 4-22, person on your left): Sit flat on the floor and place both soles of your feet together so your legs create a diamond shape (butterfly) as shown in Figure 4-22. Grasp your shins with your hands.

c. Movement (Figure 4-22, person on your right): Keep your back flat and gently lean forward to feel the stretch in your inner thighs, groin and buttocks. Hold the stretch for 15 to 30 seconds.

FIGURE 4-22. Inner thigh, groin and buttocks stretch.

Summary Questions

1. Describe a static stretch and give an example.

2. Describe a dynamic stretch and give an example.

3. Describe a PNF stretch and give an example.

4. What types of stretches are most effective during the warm-up phase of a workout?

5. What types of stretches are most effective during the cool-down phase of a workout?

References

Washington State University, *Flexibility Training*, (2016) University Recreation Exercise.

OrthoInfo, *Warm Up, Cool Down and be Flexible*, American Academy of Orthopaedic Surgeons, January 2012

Mayo Clinic, Healthy Lifestyle, *Stretching: Focus on Flexibility*, Stretching Essentials, March 2014

Blahnik, J. Full Body Flexibility, 2nd Edition, *Types of Stretching*.

Goldman, R., Healthline, *Ballistic Stretching: Is It Safe?*, August 2014

Millar, A.L., *Improving Your Flexibility and Balance*, American College of Sports Medicine, February 2012

Reynolds, G., *The Right Way To Stretch Before Exercise*, The New York Times, January 2016

Cassetty, J., Syatt, J., *Best Warm Up Exercises Before a Workout*, Greatist, October 2015

Exercise and Physical Activity: Your Everyday Guide from the National Institute on Aging, *Sample Exercise—Flexibility*, January 2016

Web Sites

http://www.acsm.org
American College of Sports Medicine

http://www.ncoa.org/improve-health/center-for-healthy-aging/content-library/ExerciseGuide_FINAL_Aug2010_0.pdf
Exercise: A Guide From the National Institute on Aging

http://orthoinfo.aaos.org
American Academy of Orthopaedic Surgeons

http://www2.gsu.edu/~wwwfit/flexibility.html
Georgia State University: Flexibility

http://www.mayoclinic.org/healthy-lifestyle/fitness/in-depth/stretching/art-20047631

http://www.ideafit.com/fitness-library/stretching-research-retrospective

http://exercise.wsu.edu/flexibility/default.aspx

https://search.wsu.edu/Default.aspx?cx=002970099942160159670%3Ayqxxz06m1b0&cof=FORID%3A11&sa=Search&q=exercise+guidelines

https://www.nia.nih.gov/health/publication/exercise-physical-activity/sample-exercises-flexibility

chapter 5

Health-Related Fitness
Body Composition

by Ritchie Shuford, M.A.

Introduction

The topics of health-related fitness, overweight and obesity are in the news almost daily. Ironically, in a society in which being fit, trim, and lean seems to be highly desirable, the evidence of overweight and obesity remains in epidemic proportion. The Centers for Disease Control and Prevention (CDC) report that almost 17% of the United States' children between the ages of two and nineteen and 66% of the adult population are overweight or obese. In economic terms, it is estimated that this collision course with our bodies will cost over $334 billion, or 21% of the United States' health-care spending.

Beginning at the age of 25, the average United States' male and female will gain approximately one pound of weight per year. So, by the age of 65, the typical U.S. citizen will have gained some 40 pounds of weight. Due to the typical reduction of physical activity in our present-day society, each year the average person also loses a half-pound of lean tissue. This trend over a 40-year period has resulted in the average person's fat gain of 60 pounds, accompanied by a 20-pound loss of lean body mass. These gradual changes are difficult to detect unless body composition is regularly assessed.

Body composition is considered to be the fat and nonfat components of the human body. The fat component of the body is referred to as fat mass or percent body fat. The nonfat component is referred to as lean body mass. Body composition is the only health-related fitness component that is not assessed using a performance-related measure (number of push-ups, 2-mile walk time, etc.).

Essential and Nonessential Fat

The total amount of fat in the human body is classified into two basic categories: essential fat and nonessential fat (storage fats). Essential fat constitutes about 2–5% of the total weight in men and 8–12% in women. The fat percentages are higher in women due to gender-specific fat areas, such as the uterus, breast tissue, and other gender-related protective fat deposits. Essential fat is stored in the marrow of bones, as well as in the heart, lungs, liver, spleen, kidneys, intestines, muscles, and lipid-rich tissues of the central nervous system. This fat is required for normal physiologic functioning. It isn't quite clear whether this fat is expendable or serves as a reserve. For females, an exceptionally low body fat percentage may be a cause for concern. Amenorrhea may occur at fat levels of less than 10% and even 11–16% for some women. National standards indicate that males should not possess less than 5% body fat and females less than 10%.

Storage fat, or nonessential fat, is the other category which consists of fat that accumulates in excess amounts that result in over-fatness or obesity. Just as the percentage of body fat should not drop too low, neither should it get too high. There is a desirable range of body fatness that is associated with sound metabolic fitness and overall health and wellness.

Body Mass Index

Body mass index (BMI) is a non-invasive technique scientists and physicians use to determine thinness and excessive fatness. However, it is not always accurate for some groups because BMI doesn't distinguish between fat weight and fat-free weight. For example, a football lineman with more muscle mass than an average person may be classified as overweight or obese. BMI can be found by dividing the weight in kilograms by the square of the height in meters. The following four-step example is for a person who is 6 feet (72 inches) and weighs 200 pounds.

1. Divide body weight in pounds by 2.2 to convert weight to kilograms:
   $$200 \div 2.2 = 90.91$$

2. Multiply height in inches by 0.0254 to convert height to meters:
   $$72 \times 0.0254 = 1.83$$

BMI	19	20	21	22	23	24	25	26	27	28	29	30	35	40
HEIGHT (inches)							WEIGHT (pounds)							
58	91	95	100	105	110	115	119	124	129	134	138	143	167	191
59	94	99	104	109	114	119	124	128	133	138	143	148	173	198
60	97	102	107	112	118	123	128	133	138	143	148	153	179	204
61	100	106	111	116	121	127	132	137	143	148	153	158	185	211
62	104	109	115	120	125	131	136	142	147	153	158	164	191	218
63	107	113	118	124	130	135	141	146	152	158	163	169	197	225
64	110	116	122	128	134	140	145	151	157	163	169	174	203	233
65	114	120	126	132	138	144	150	156	162	168	174	180	210	240
66	117	124	130	136	142	148	155	161	167	173	179	185	216	247
67	121	127	134	140	147	153	159	166	172	178	185	191	223	255
68	125	131	138	144	151	158	164	171	177	184	190	197	230	263
69	128	135	142	149	155	162	169	176	182	189	196	203	237	270
70	132	139	146	153	160	167	174	181	188	195	202	209	243	278
71	136	143	150	157	165	172	179	186	193	200	207	215	250	286
72	140	147	155	162	169	177	184	191	199	206	213	221	258	294
73	144	151	159	166	174	182	189	197	204	212	219	227	265	303
74	148	155	163	171	179	187	194	202	210	218	225	233	272	311
75	152	160	168	176	184	192	200	208	216	224	232	240	279	319
76	156	164	172	180	189	197	205	213	221	230	238	246	287	328

3. Multiply the result of step 2 by itself to get the square of the height measurement:

    1.83 × 1.83 = 3.35

4. Divide the result of step 1 by the result of step 3 to determine BMI:

    90.91 ÷ 3.35 = 27.14

To calculate BMI

$$BMI = \frac{Weight\ (kg)}{Height\ (m)^2}$$

According to the BMI scale, the lowest risk for chronic disease is in the 19 to 25 range. Individuals who possess a BMI between 25 and 30 are classified as overweight, those above 30 are obese, and those below 19 are underweight.

BMI Reference Chart

WEIGHT CATEGORY	BMI RANGE
Normal weight	19 to <25
Overweight	25 to <30
Obese	30 to <35
Seriously obese	≥ 35

Assessing Body Fatness

Body composition is considered to be the relative amount of fat and lean body mass. The normal range is 20–25 percent for women and 12–20 percent for men. When the body fat exceeds 25 percent for women and/or 20 percent for men, the risk of chronic disease rises drastically. There are several methods used in assessing body fatness, but there are some advantages and disadvantages associated with each.

Hydrostatic, or underwater weighing, was once considered the leading standard of body composition analysis. Hydrostatic measurements are based on the assumption that the density and specific gravity of lean tissue is greater than that of fat tissue. Thus, lean tissue will sink in water and fat tissue will float. However, there are several limitations to the hydrostatic weighing method. The equipment required to perform hydrostatic measurements is bulky and maintenance-intense. The total test procedure may require 45 minutes to one hour. A large 100-gallon tank of water must be maintained at a constant temperature.

Another type of body composition measure that uses the same principles as underwater weighing is air displacement plethysmography (ADP). Subjects sit in a sealed BOD POD and displace air instead of water to determine body volume. Body volume is combined with body weight (mass) to then calculate the percentage of body fat and lean body mass (LBM). Standard conversion tables are then applied.

Body composition is also estimated by magnetic resonance imaging (MRI) and computed tomography (CT), which are quite costly. Dual-energy X-ray absorptiometry (DXA) is a newer, less complex and more efficient way to analyze body composition. It differentiates among bone, other lean tissue and fat by applying dual-energy scanning.

Bioelectrical impedance analysis (BIA) is yet another method to measure body composition. This procedure measures the rate at which a small amount of electric current flows through the body between electrodes placed on the wrist and ankle. Fat tissue does not conduct electricity as well as lean tissue; it resists or impedes the current. Electrolytes containing fluids, such as fluid found mostly in lean body tissues, is less likely to cause resistance. The impedance reading allows the researcher to calculate total body water and then estimate total lean body mass and body fatness.

One of the most common and more practical methods of assessing body fatness is the use of a skinfold caliper device to measure the thickness of subcutaneous fat stores at multiple body sites. Skinfold measurements are less complicated and not nearly as costly as other assessment procedures. The more sites that are measured on the body, the more accurate the body fatness estimate will be. However, measurements of two or three skinfolds have been shown to be reasonably accurate and can be administered in a relatively short time.

- Tricep fold: one-half the distance between the tip of the shoulder and the tip of the elbow

- Iliac crest skinfold: top front of the iliac crest

- Thigh skinfold: front of the thigh midway between the hip and the knee

- Chest skinfold: to the right of the right nipple (one-half the distance from the midline of the side and the nipple)

- Abdominal skinfold: one inch to the right of the navel

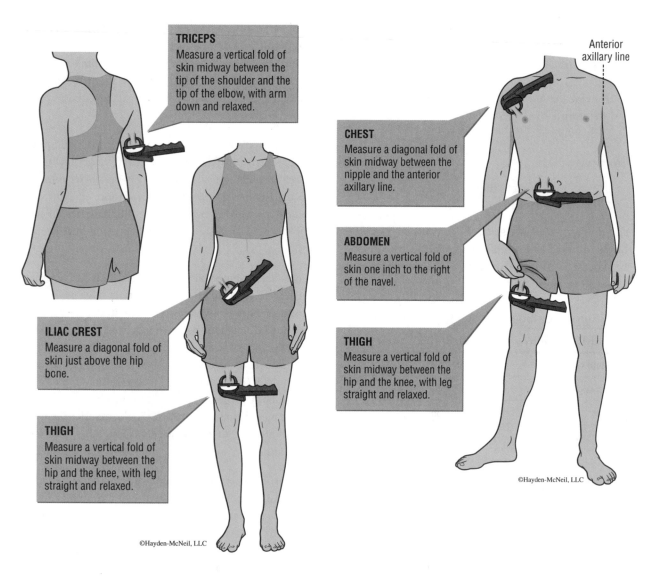

TRICEPS
Measure a vertical fold of skin midway between the tip of the shoulder and the tip of the elbow, with arm down and relaxed.

ILIAC CREST
Measure a diagonal fold of skin just above the hip bone.

THIGH
Measure a vertical fold of skin midway between the hip and the knee, with leg straight and relaxed.

©Hayden-McNeil, LLC

CHEST
Measure a diagonal fold of skin midway between the nipple and the anterior axillary line.

ABDOMEN
Measure a vertical fold of skin one inch to the right of the navel.

THIGH
Measure a vertical fold of skin midway between the hip and the knee, with leg straight and relaxed.

Anterior axillary line

©Hayden-McNeil, LLC

FIGURE 5-1. Skinfold locations for women.

FIGURE 5-2. Skinfold locations for men.

Body Fat Percentage Classification

CLASSIFICATION	PERCENT FAT	
	WOMEN	MEN
Essential Fat (very lean)	10–13%	2–5%
Athletes (lean low)	14–20%	6–13%
Fitness (leaner than average)	21–24%	14–17%
Healthy (average)	25–31%	18–24%
Obese (fat)	32% and higher	25% and higher

Table 5-1. Percent Body Fat Estimations for Women—Jackson and Pollock Formula

SUM OF SKINFOLDS (mm)	AGE GROUPS								
	Under 22	23–27	28–32	33–37	38–42	43–47	48–52	53–57	over 57
23–25	9.7	9.9	10.2	10.4	10.7	10.9	11.2	11.4	11.7
26–28	11.0	11.2	11.5	11.7	12.0	12.3	12.5	12.7	13.0
29–31	12.3	12.5	12.8	13.0	13.3	13.5	13.8	14.0	14.3
32–34	13.6	13.8	14.0	14.3	14.5	14.8	15.0	15.3	15.5
35–37	14.8	15.0	15.3	15.5	15.8	16.0	16.3	16.5	16.8
38–40	16.0	16.3	16.5	16.7	17.0	17.2	17.5	17.7	18.0
41–43	17.2	17.4	17.7	17.9	18.2	18.4	18.7	18.9	19.2
44–46	18.3	18.6	18.8	19.1	19.3	19.6	19.8	20.1	20.3
47–49	19.5	19.7	20.0	20.2	20.5	20.7	21.0	21.2	21.5
50–52	20.6	20.8	21.1	21.3	21.6	21.8	22.1	22.3	22.6
53–55	21.7	21.9	22.1	22.4	22.6	22.9	23.1	23.4	23.6
56–58	22.7	23.0	23.2	23.4	23.7	23.9	24.2	24.4	24.7
59–61	23.7	24.0	24.2	24.5	24.7	25.0	25.2	25.5	25.7
62–64	24.7	25.0	25.2	25.5	25.7	26.0	26.7	26.4	26.7
65–67	25.7	25.9	26.2	26.4	26.7	26.9	27.2	27.4	27.7
68–70	26.6	26.9	27.1	27.4	27.6	27.9	28.1	28.4	28.6
71–73	27.5	27.8	28.0	28.3	28.5	28.8	29.0	29.3	29.5
74–76	28.4	28.7	28.9	29.2	29.4	29.7	29.9	30.2	30.4
77–79	29.3	29.5	29.8	30.0	30.3	30.5	30.8	31.0	31.3
80–82	30.1	30.4	30.6	30.9	31.1	31.4	31.6	31.9	32.1
83–85	30.9	31.2	31.4	31.7	31.9	32.2	32.4	32.7	32.9
86–88	31.7	32.0	32.2	32.5	32.7	32.9	33.2	33.4	33.7
89–91	32.5	32.7	33.0	33.2	33.5	33.7	33.9	34.2	34.4
92–94	33.2	33.4	33.7	33.9	34.2	34.4	34.7	34.9	35.2
95–97	33.9	34.1	34.4	34.6	34.9	35.1	35.4	35.6	35.9
98–100	34.6	34.8	35.1	35.3	35.5	35.8	36.0	36.3	36.5
101–103	35.3	35.4	35.7	35.9	36.2	36.4	36.7	36.9	37.2
104–106	35.8	36.1	36.3	36.6	36.8	37.1	37.3	37.5	37.8
107–109	36.4	36.7	36.9	37.1	37.4	37.6	37.9	38.1	38.4
110–112	37.0	37.2	37.5	37.7	38.0	38.2	38.5	38.7	38.9
113–115	37.5	37.8	38.0	38.2	38.5	38.7	39.0	39.2	39.5
116–118	38.0	38.3	38.5	38.8	39.0	39.3	39.5	39.7	40.0
119–121	38.5	38.7	39.0	39.2	39.5	39.7	40.0	40.2	40.5
122–124	39.0	39.2	39.4	39.7	39.9	40.2	40.4	40.7	40.9
125–127	39.4	39.6	39.9	40.1	40.4	40.6	40.9	41.1	41.4
128–130	39.8	40.0	40.3	40.5	40.8	41.0	41.3	41.5	41.8

Source: Jackson, A.S. & Pollock, M.L.: Practical Assessment of Body Composition. *The Physician and Sportsmedicine*, 13:76–90, 1985.

Table 5-2. Percent Body Fat Estimations for Men—Jackson and Pollock Formula

SUM OF SKINFOLDS (mm)	AGE GROUPS								
	Under 22	23–27	28–32	33–37	38–42	43–47	48–52	53–57	over 57
8–10	1.3	1.8	2.3	2.9	3.4	3.9	4.5	5.0	5.5
11–13	2.2	2.8	3.3	3.9	4.4	4.9	5.5	6.0	6.5
14–16	3.2	3.8	A.3	4.8	5.4	5.9	6.4	7.0	7.5
17–19	4.2	4.7	5.3	5.8	6.3	6.9	7.4	8.0	8.5
20–22	5.1	5.7	6.2	6.8	7.3	7.9	8.4	8.9	9.5
23–25	6.1	6.6	7.2	7.7	8.3	8.8	9.4	9.9	10.5
26–28	7.0	7.6	8.1	8.7	9.2	9.8	10.3	10.9	11.4
29–31	8.0	8.5	9.1	9.6	10.2	10.7	11.3	11.8	12.4
32–34	8.9	9.4	10.0	10.5	11.1	11.6	12.2	12.8	13.3
35–37	9.8	10.4	10.9	11.5	12.0	12.6	13.1	13.7	14.3
38–40	10.7	11.3	11.8	12.4	12.9	13.5	14.1	14.6	15.2
41–43	11.6	12.2	12.7	13.3	13.8	14.4	15.0	15.5	16.1
44–46	12.5	13.1	13.6	14.2	14.7	15.3	15.9	16.4	17.0
47–49	13.4	13.9	14.5	15.1	15.6	16.2	16.8	17.3	17.9
50–52	14.3	14.8	15.4	15.9	16.5	17.1	17.6	18.2	18.8
53–55	15.1	15.7	16.2	16.8	17.4	17.9	18.5	19.1	19.7
56–58	16.0	16.5	17.1	17.7	18.2	18.8	19.4	20.0	20.5
59–61	16.9	17.4	17.9	18.5	19.1	19.7	20.2	20.8	21.4
62–64	17.6	18.2	18.8	19.4	19.9	20.5	21.1	21.7	22.2
65–67	18.5	19.0	19.6	20.2	20.8	21.3	21.9	22.5	23.1
68–70	19.3	19.9	20.4	21.0	21.6	22.2	22.7	23.3	23.9
71–73	20.1	20.7	21.2	21.8	22.4	23.0	23.6	24.1	24.7
74–76	20.9	21.5	22.0	22.6	23.2	23.8	24.4	25.0	25.5
77–79	21.7	22.2	22.8	23.4	24.0	24.6	25.2	25.8	26.3
80–82	22.4	23.0	23.6	24.2	24.8	25.4	25.9	26.5	27.1
83–85	23.2	23.8	24.4	25.0	25.5	26.1	26.7	27.3	27.9
86–88	24.0	24.5	25.1	25.7	26.3	26.9	27.5	28.1	28.7
89–91	24.7	25.3	25.9	26.5	27.1	27.6	28.2	28.8	29.4
92–94	25.4	26.0	26.6	27.2	27.8	28.4	29.0	29.6	30.2
95–97	26.1	26.7	27.3	27.9	28.5	29.1	29.7	30.3	30.9
98–100	26.9	27.4	28.0	28.6	29.2	29.8	30.4	31.0	31.6
101–103	27.5	28.1	28.7	29.3	29.9	30.5	31.1	31.7	32.3
104–106	28.2	28.8	29.4	30.0	30.6	31.2	31.8	32.4	33.0
107–109	28.9	29.5	30.1	30.7	31.3	31.9	32.5	33.1	33.7
110–112	29.6	30.2	30.8	31.4	32.0	32.6	33.2	33.8	34.4
113–115	30.2	30.8	31.4	32.0	32.6	33.2	33.8	34.5	35.1
116–118	30.9	31.5	32.1	32.7	33.3	33.9	34.5	35.1	35.7
119–121	31.5	32.1	32.7	33.3	33.9	34.5	35.1	35.7	36.4
122–124	32.1	32.7	33.3	33.9	34.5	35.1	35.8	36.4	37.0
125–127	32.7	33.3	33.9	34.5	35.1	35.8	36.4	37.0	37.6

Summary Questions

1. Identify the five components of health-related fitness. What is the only non-performance component?

2. Based on what you have read, identify five things that you might practice to impact your body composition.

3. Why might women possess a higher percent body fat than men?

4. How do you calculate Body Mass Index?

References

American College of Sports Medicine. (2011). *ACSM's Complete Guide to Health & Fitness: Physical Activity and Nutritional Guidelines*. Champaign, IL: Human Kinetics.

American College of Sports Medicine. (2003). *ACSM's Fitness Book*. Champaign, IL: Human Kinetics.

American College of Sports Medicine. (2009). *ACSM's Guidelines for Exercise Testing & Prescription*. 8th Ed. Philadelphia, PA: Lippincott, Williams & Wilkins.

American College of Sports Medicine (2010). *ACSM's Health-Related Fitness Manual*. 8th Ed. Philadelphia, PA: Lippincott, Williams & Wilkins.

American College of Sports Medicine. (2009). *ACSM's Resource Manual for Guidelines for Exercise Testing & Prescription*. 6th Ed. Philadelphia, PA: Lippincott, Williams & Wilkins.

Bouchard, C.; Blair, S.N. & Haskell, W. (2012). *Physical Activity and Health*. Champaign, IL: Human Kinetics.

Chan, R.S. & Woo, J. (2010). Prevention of Overweight and Obesity. *International Journal of Environmental Research and Public Health*. 7(3):765–783.

Corbin, C. et al. (2011). *Concepts of Physical Fitness*. New York, NY: McGraw-Hill.

Dahm, D. & Smith, J. (2005). *Mayo Clinic Fitness for Everybody*. Rochester, MN. Mayo Clinic.

Finkestein, E.A. (2010). Individual and Aggregate Years of Life Lost Associated with Overweight and Obesity. *Obesity* 18(2):33–339.

Heyward, V. & Wagner, D.R. (2004). *Applied Body Composition Assessment*. Champaign, IL: Human Kinetics.

Jackson, A.S. & Pollock, M.L. Practical Assessment of Body Composition. *Physician and Sportsmedicine*. 13:76–90, 1985.

Lee, I. et.al. (2010). Physical Activity and Weight Gain Prevention. *Journal of the American Medical Association*. 303(12):1173–1179.

Web Sites

http://www.acsm.org
American College of Sports Medicine

http://www.aahperd.org
American Alliance of Health, Physical Education, Recreation and Dance

http://www.mayoclinic.com
Mayo Clinic

http://www.cdc.gov
Centers for Disease Control and Prevention

http://www.hopkinsmedicine.org
Johns Hopkins Medicine

http://www.surgeongeneral.gov/initiatives/healthy-fit-nation/obesityvision2010.pdf
Surgeon General

http://www.letsmove.gov
Let's Move Campaign

http://www.shapeup.org
Shape Up America

Section Three

Wellness

Wellness reflects how one feels about life, as well as one's ability to function effectively. Wellness is an expanded idea of health. It is the ability to live life fully, with vitality and meaning. True wellness is determined by the decisions you make about how to live your life. There are seven interrelated dimensions of wellness. The strength of each of these dimensions will vary at different stages in an individual's life. All must be developed in order to achieve wellness.

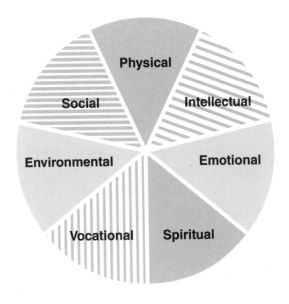

Seven Dimensions of Wellness

Physical Dimension—Keeping your body functioning at its maximum capacity over the entire lifespan.

Intellectual Dimension—Embracing lifetime learning.

Emotional Dimension—Experiencing and expressing a wide range of feelings and coping with life's occurrences.

Spiritual Dimension—Reflecting upon what inspires and motivates each individual intrinsically.

Vocational Dimension—Identifying and using skills, abilities, and interests to incorporate into your life's work.

Environmental Dimension—Acknowledging the interdependence between man and earth and other living beings.

Social Dimension—Being able to create and sustain relationships with family, friends, peers, and acquaintances over time.

Lifestyle Management

An individual makes healthy decisions through either enhancing wellness or reducing risks. For lifestyle management, an internal focus of control is an advantage. If an individual has an internal focus of control, they know that the source of responsibility for the events in one's life is oneself, instead of forces outside of their control. The choices you make can have a direct impact in prevention of the leading causes of death (heart disease, cancer, stroke, accidents, etc.) in the United States.

Examples of Lifestyle Management That Contribute to Wellness

1. Being physically active

2. Eating a healthy diet

3. Maintaining a healthy body weight

4. Managing stress effectively

5. Avoiding the use of tobacco and reducing or eliminating alcohol

6. Protecting yourself from disease and injury

7. Using medical assistance when necessary

8. Recycling

9. Using morals and ethics in everyday decisions

10. Building healthy relationships

11. Learning new things

12. Balancing work and social life

chapter 6

Wellness
Nutrition

by Kari Lewis, Ed.D.

The average American today will consume more calories a day than in the past and yet the nutrient content of these calories is lower. We have become a population of overfed, undernourished, and physically inactive people largely due to the increases in fast food consumption, decreases in physically taxing jobs, and the desire to get a proportion of food worth what we pay for it. Over the past 20 years there has been an increase in obesity rates across the United States. National obesity trends show that 33.8% of U.S. adults are obese. Additionally, 17% of Americans aged 2–19 years old are obese. This comes as no surprise when a single dollar purchases 1,200 calories of cookies or potato chips, yet only 250 calories of carrots. Energy-dense foods are the least expensive and resilient to inflation, so it's no wonder obesity rates continue to increase.

What you eat affects your energy level, well-being, and overall health. This chapter will explain the basic principles of nutrition. The first step toward healthier eating is to develop a better understanding of nutrients, where they come from, what they do in the body, and how much of each you need. The next step will be to translate your nutritional knowledge into a diet consisting of appropriate amounts of foods that are both affordable and enjoyable!

Dietary Components

Most individuals consume too much of one nutrient and not enough of another. Energy expenditure levels require your nutrient intake to be proportionate. If your intake is unbalanced, you run the risk of reducing your energy levels, impairing body processes, and increasing the risk of developing several chronic diseases or conditions. Nutrients are divided into six classes, which we refer to as essential nutrients. They are carbohydrates, proteins, fats, vitamins, minerals, and water. Nutrients are obtained by the ingestion and subsequent absorption of food through digestion. Food is chewed, mixed with digestive enzymes, and moved through the digestive tract. The nutrients are

6

Chapter
Six

broken down into small molecules that can be absorbed into the bloodstream and dispersed throughout the body.

The six essential nutrients can be broken down into two categories: **macronutrients** and **micronutrients**. Macronutrients are needed in relatively large amounts. Of the six essential nutrients, carbohydrates, protein, fat and water are macronutrients. Three of these provide a source of energy for the body that is expressed as a **kilocalorie**, more typically referred to as a **Calorie**. One kilocalorie is representative of the amount of energy it takes to raise the temperature of one liter of water 1 degree Celsius. A calorie can be a term used to determine the amount of energy burned through physical activity. A person needs a certain amount of calories to meet his or her needs on a daily basis. The three nutrients that provide energy are:

- Carbohydrates = 4 calories per gram

- Protein = 4 calories per gram

- Fat = 9 calories per gram

Water does not contain calories but it is needed in large amounts for the body to function; therefore, it is considered a macronutrient. The goal of a well-balanced diet is for both calories ingested and calories burned to be balanced. Most of us do not need extra calories to meet our daily energy needs. Regardless of the source, calories ingested that are not required for our energy needs are typically converted to fat and stored in the body.

Micronutrients, which are vitamins and minerals, are needed in lesser quantities yet still are essential to maintaining and regulating various processes and reactions that take place within the body. Micronutrients provide the compounds that enable the reactions that cause the release of energy from macronutrients. It is essential that your diet consist of nutrients from all six essential nutrients in order for the body to function properly.

Carbohydrates

During high intensity exercise, muscles get most of their energy from **carbohydrates**. When ingested, carbohydrates are broken down into glucose, which circulates in the blood and is a readily available energy source for the cells. Any glucose that is not used is stored as glycogen in the liver and skeletal muscles. When energy is needed again, the glycogen can be converted back to glucose for use. There are limits as to how much glucose can be stored as glycogen, so any excess is converted and stored as fat.

Carbohydrates are classified into two groups: simple and complex. **Simple carbohydrates** are defined structurally as monosaccharides (glucose, fructose, galactose) and disaccharides (sucrose, maltose, lactose). Simple carbohydrates occur naturally in fruits, honey, sweet potatoes, milk products, and some cereal products. They are also added to foods during processing and preparation to add calories and taste but few other essential nutrients.

Complex carbohydrates, which include starches and fiber, are made up of long chains of monosaccharides linked together called polysaccharides. Starches are found in a variety of plants, especially grains (wheat, rice, oats, barley), legumes (beans, peas, and lentils), and tubers (potatoes and yams). Most vegetables contain a mixture of simple and complex carbohydrates. Fiber is a non digestible carbohydrate found in fruits, vegetables, and grains. Rather than being digested like starches, fiber moves through the intestinal tract and provides bulk in the large intestines to aid in elimination of waste. As with all other nutrients, too much can be contraindicated. The daily recommended amount of fiber for adults is 20–35 grams, which can be found in fresh fruits, vegetables, and foods made from whole grains.

When carbohydrates are broken down after a snack or meal, there is a spike not only in blood glucose levels, but in insulin levels as well. Some carbohydrates cause an immediate spike in blood insulin, while others result in a slower insulin release. The effect carbohydrates have on the speed of insulin released into the bloodstream is known as the **Glycemic Index**. High glycemic index foods (increased speed of insulin release) include simple sugars, white rice, and potatoes. Low glycemic index foods (decreased speed of insulin release) include whole grains, vegetables, etc.

The recommended intake of carbohydrates should be between 45–65% of total calories. This is about 300 g/day for a person who weights 154 pounds. Very active individuals or athletes should increase carbohydrate intake to 60–70% or 400–600 g of their total daily calorie intake.

Protein

Amino acids are the basic units or building blocks for protein. There are 20 different amino acids, eight of which (nine in children and stressed older adults) are "essential" amino acids that must be obtained through the ingestion of foods. The remaining 12 are considered non-essential because they can be manufactured by the body. Individuals who are considered vegetarians must consider these parameters when selecting daily food choices.

Proteins are important for tissue growth and repair, and also regulate the acid–base quality of body fluids. Proteins provide 4 kilocalories per gram, but they are considered an inefficient fuel source.

Proteins are classified as complete or incomplete. **Complete** protein sources provide all the essential amino acids. **Incomplete** proteins lack one or more of the essential amino acids. Eggs are a perfect protein, to which all other food sources are compared. In addition, meat, dairy products, and soy are complete proteins. Incomplete proteins include whole grains, legumes, and rice. Quinoa is a grain grown in South America that contains all essential amino acids; therefore, it is the only grain we know of that is considered a complete protein.

The recommended daily intake of protein for adults is 0.8 g per kilogram (kg) of body weight. To find out how much protein you require, divide your body weight by 2.2 and multiply by .8. Example: (140 divided by 2.2) $\times$ .8 = 50.9 g protein. (Protein needs can also be calculated by multiplying .36 g per pound of body weight.) The average individual should get 10–15% of daily caloric intake from protein. Endurance athletes require 1.2–1.4 g per kilogram (kg) of body weight; strength athletes require 1.6–1.7 g per kg.

Fats

Fats are also an important energy source for our bodies, especially during low-intensity exercise and while we are resting. Fat is a dense fuel source, providing 9 kilocalories per gram. In addition to being an energy source, fats have other important functions in the body. Fats provide cushion and support for the body's vital organs, they help our bodies retain heat by acting as insulation, and they are needed for the absorption of fat-soluble vitamins. Most importantly, fats provide foods with texture and flavor and help us to feel satiated after a meal.

Of the three types of fats common in foods (triglycerides, phospholipids, and sterols), triglycerides make up about 95% of the fat we eat. Triglycerides are also the form of fat commonly found in the body. Triglycerides have different fatty acid structures that can result in a different type of fat based on their length, level of saturation, and shape. Different types of fatty acids have different characteristics and different effects on your body. Regardless of the type of fat, the small intestine is where the major part of fat digestion occurs.

The designation of saturation is based on the number of double bonds in the fatty acid chain. Saturated fats have no double bonds; therefore, they can be packed more tightly, which is why most saturated fats are solid at room temperature. The unsaturated fats, monounsaturated and polyunsaturated, contain one or more than one double bond in the chain and are typically in the *cis* shape. These fats tend to be liquid at room temperature because they cannot be packed tightly together.

Another form of fat that occurs naturally, but is prominent in our food due to a man-made process, is *trans* fat. *Trans* **fats** are made by heating unsaturated fats to remove some or all of the double bonds, resulting in a chain similar or close to that of saturated fat. *Trans* fats are used especially in processed crackers and snacks in order to prolong shelf-life. If you read *hydrogenated* or *partially hydrogenated* oil in the list of ingredients, the product contains *trans* fat. Because *trans* fats are as great a concern as saturated fats, food manufacturers are now required to list the amount of *trans* fat in their products. As a result, there has been a movement to reduce or eliminate *trans* fats from many products.

Table 6-1. Sources of Triglycerides

TYPE OF FAT	FOOD SOURCES
Saturated	Animal sources: cheese, whole milk, half and half, lard, bacon, hot dogs Tropical oils: palm oil, coconut oil
Monounsaturated	Olive, peanut, canola, and avocado oils
Polyunsaturated (omega-3 sources)	Corn, safflower, sunflower, soybean, sesame, and vegetable oils
Trans fat	Processed foods: snack crackers, cookies, cereals

The majority of our fat intake should be from monounsaturated and polyunsaturated fats. One polyunsaturated fat has been linked to reducing many heart-related diseases.

This fat is *Omega-3* fatty acids, which are considered essential because the body cannot make them. Omega-3 fatty acids are found in fish and certain plants and nuts.

Cholesterol is a sterol fat found in foods of animal origin or synthesized within the body. Cholesterol is not found in vegetable food sources and is negligible in egg whites and skim milk. The highest content of cholesterol is found in egg yolks. Other foods that contain large amounts are red meat, organ meats (liver, kidney, and brain), and dairy products such as ice cream, butter, cheese, and whole milk.

In the body, we are typically concerned about High Density Lipoproteins (HDL) and Low Density Lipoproteins (LDL). HDL is produced in the liver and small intestine and is known as the "good" cholesterol because it protects against heart disease by removing cholesterol from the artery wall and carrying it to the liver, where it is converted into bile and excreted through the intestine. LDL is known as the "bad" cholesterol because it deposits cholesterol on the artery walls that can build up, resulting in "plaque" formation, which causes limited or stopped blood flow. *Trans* fats, like saturated fats, increase LDL levels and decrease HDL, contributing to the onset of heart disease. Exercise has a positive effect by increasing HDL levels.

In the United States, our dietary fat intake on average is about 40–50% of our total caloric intake. The American Heart Association suggests a diet of less than 30% of total calories from fat, with saturated, monounsaturated, and polyunsaturated fats making up 10% each. Cholesterol is continually manufactured by the body and therefore should be limited to less than 300 mg per day.

> **DID YOU KNOW?**
>
> Americans spend over $140 billion on fast food each year! The number of fast food chains in the U.S. has increased by over 1000% since 1970. A cheeseburger happy meal with fries and a Sprite contains 640 calories and 24 grams of fat, that's over half of the total calories many children should be eating in a day! And the average serving size for burgers, fries, and sodas has more than tripled since the 1970s! In a 2011 study published by the Journal of the American Medical Association, laboratory measurements compared the calories in 269 food items with the restaurants' stated calories. Researchers found that 19% of food items had at least 100 calories more than listed and only 7% of the 269 foods tested were within 10 calories of what the restaurants stated.

Vitamins

Vitamins are water-soluble or fat-soluble organic substances required in small amounts to regulate important processes in the body and to perform very specific functions for the metabolism of carbohydrates, fats, and proteins for energy.

The fat-soluble vitamins, A, D, E, and K, are stored in the liver and fat cells of adipose tissue and are retained for a relatively long time in the tissue. Daily consumption of these vitamins is unnecessary and could result in toxicity. They are absorbed with dietary fat in the intestines.

Water-soluble vitamins, B vitamins and vitamin C, dissolve in water and are associated with the water parts of food and body tissue. Water-soluble vitamins are absorbed through the intestinal wall directly into the bloodstream. Water-soluble vitamins cannot be stored in the body and, if not used, will be flushed out in the urine. Your diet must contain these on a regular basis.

Table 6-2. Fat-Soluble Vitamins

VITAMIN	FUNCTION	SOURCES
Vitamin A	Important in vision and resistance to infection	Leafy green vegetables, yellow and orange vegetables, milk, butter, cheese
Vitamin D	Growth of bones and calcium absorption	Eggs, dairy products, fortified milk, fish liver oil
Vitamin E	Antioxidant* to prevent cell damage by free radicals	Seeds, leafy green vegetables, margarine
Vitamin K	Blood clotting	Green leafy vegetables, cereals

*Antioxidants are compounds such as vitamins C, E, beta-carotene, and the mineral selenium, which prevent oxygen from combining with other substances so that it may cause damage; thought to play a role in preventing heart disease and cancer.

Table 6-3. Water-Soluble Vitamins

VITAMIN	FUNCTION	SOURCES
Thiamine (B1)	Releases energy from carbohydrates during metabolism; growth and muscle tone	Fortified cereals and oatmeal, rice, pasta, meats, whole grains, and liver
Riboflavin (B3)	Releases energy from protein, fat, and carbohydrates during metabolism	Whole grains, green leafy vegetables, organ meats, milk and cheese
Pyridoxine (B6)	Builds body tissue and aids in metabolism of protein	Fish, poultry, lean meats, bananas, dried beans, whole grains, avocado
Cobalamin (B12)	All development and functioning of the nervous system; protein and fat metabolism	Meats, milk, products, and seafood
Folate (folic acid)	Genetic material development and red blood cell production	Green leafy vegetables, organ meats, dried peas, beans, and lentils
Niacin	Carbohydrate, fat, and protein metabolism	Meat, poultry, fish, potatoes, dairy products, eggs, enriched cereals
Vitamin C (ascorbic acid)	Bone, cartilage, muscle, and blood vessel structure; maintains capillaries and gums; aids in absorption of iron	Citrus fruit, berries, vegetables—especially peppers

Minerals

Minerals differ from the other essential nutrients in that they are not broken down during digestion or absorption—they maintain their structure in all environments. Minerals have many functions in the body. First, they help maintain proper fluid balance and normal cell and muscle activity. Second, they provide structure in the formation of bones and teeth. Third, they help maintain normal heart rhythm, muscle contractions, and nerve impulse conduction. Fourth, they regulate metabolism.

Our bodies can't make minerals, so we must get them through our food. There are 18 minerals known to be useful to the body, and seven are considered essential and have FDA requirements. Minerals are divided into two groups, major and trace, based on how much is found in our bodies and how much we need to consume through our diet.

Table 6-4. Major Minerals: Greater than 100 mg per Day

MINERAL	FUNCTION	SOURCES
Calcium	Bone and teeth formation; blood clotting; nerve transmission; important for weight maintenance	Milk, cheese, dark green vegetables, dried legumes
Sodium	Acid–base balance; body water balance; nerve function	Salt
Potassium	Acid–base balance; fluid balance; nerve transmission	Leafy vegetables, cantaloupe, lima beans, potatoes, bananas, milk, meats
Chloride	Acid–base balance; fluid balance; nerve transmission	Salt
Magnesium	Strengthen bones; release of energy	Nuts, eggs, whole grain cereals, leafy green vegetables, seeds, beans, bananas
Phosphorus	Works with calcium to strengthen bones	Dairy products, meat, poultry, eggs, whole grain cereals, legumes
Sulfur	Component of B vitamins thiamine and biotin; helps to stabilize the shape of proteins	Synthesized from protein-containing foods

Trace minerals are required in amounts less than 100 mg per day. Common trace minerals include selenium, iron, copper, zinc, fluorine, iodine, chromium, molybdenum, and manganese. Of these trace minerals, iron deficiency is common, especially in females. Iron is important for transporting oxygen to the body, which is especially important for exercise. Iron can be found in eggs, lean meat, legumes, whole grains, and dark green leafy vegetables.

Water

Water is essential for our survival. We can go weeks without food, but we can only survive a few days without water. Water has many functions. It is important in muscle contraction, nerve conduction, waste elimination, joint lubrication, nutrient transport, metabolism, and proper fluid balance.

About 50–70% of a healthy individual's body weight is water. As we age, our body water decreases. In addition, males usually have a higher percentage of their total body mass coming from water than females. This difference is due to the amount of lean muscle tissue (lean muscle is 70% water) as compared to fat tissue.

The recommended intake for females and males is 2.7 and 3.7 quarts of water each day, respectively. We get this water from liquid, food, and metabolism. It is recommended that we drink a minimum of 8 glasses of water a day. We usually consume around 1,350 mL of water in liquid, 1,000 mL from foods, especially fruits and vegetables that have a high water content, and the rest from metabolized water when food nutrients are broken down for energy. Additional water intake will be required during exercise and in hot/humid weather.

Dietary Supplements

What is a dietary supplement? A dietary supplement, as defined in the *Dietary Supplement Health and Education Act*, which became law in 1994, is any product that contains a "dietary ingredient" intended to add to the diet such as a vitamin, mineral, herb, botanical, amino acid, or enzyme. A supplement is generally taken orally as a type of pill or as a liquid and is always labeled on the front of the product as a dietary supplement. The U.S. Food and Drug Administration (FDA) does regulate supplements; however, they are regulated differently from other foods or drugs. The label of a dietary supplement or food can only claim to improve health, provide nutrient content, and structural function support. Unlike drug products that are approved by the FDA prior to marketing, dietary supplements can only be deemed misleading or not truthful and removed by the FDA after they have reached the consumer. The use of supplements is warranted in some situations, but always check with a physician before using any dietary supplement. For the general population a better choice is to incorporate a healthy diet and exercise program into their lifestyle.

Dietary Reference Intake for Macronutrients

The Food and Nutrition Board's DRI committee created a group to evaluate current information pertaining to macronutrients (carbohydrates, proteins, and fats) found in scientific literature to expand upon Dietary Reference Intake (DRI). Their goals were four-fold. First, to evaluate what foods provide the best quality macronutrients. Second, to develop intake levels that would influence good nutrition for life and decrease the risk of disease. Third, to evaluate the safety of consuming large quantities of certain macronutrients. Fourth, to specifically address macronutrient requirements for certain populations.

The DRI includes four types of nutrient standards: Adequate Intake (AI), Estimated Average Requirement (EAR), Tolerable Upper Intake Level (UL), and Recommended Dietary Allowance (RDA). DRIs are frequently reviewed and updated as new nutrition-related information becomes available. In 2002, the Institute of Medicine (IOM) published the Dietary Reference Intake for Macronutrients, designed to replace and expand upon the former RDAs (Recommended Daily Allowances) established by the Food and Nutrition Board. This report established ranges for fat, carbohydrates, and protein, and stresses the importance of a balanced diet with exercise. Highlights of the report include:

- Adults should get 45% to 65% of their calories from carbohydrates, 20% to 35% from fat, and 10% to 35% from protein. Acceptable ranges for children are similar to those for adults, except that infants and younger children need a slightly higher proportion of fat (25%–40%).

- To maintain cardiovascular health, regardless of weight, adults and children should achieve a total of at least one hour of moderately intense physical activity each day.

- Added sugars should comprise no more than 25% of total calories consumed. Added sugars are those incorporated into foods and beverages during production, which usually provide insignificant amounts of vitamins, minerals, or other essential nutrients. Major sources include soft drinks, fruit drinks, pastries, candy, and other sweets.

- The recommended intake for total fiber for adults 50 years and younger is set at 38 grams for men and 25 grams for women, while for men and women over

50 it is 30 and 21 grams per day, respectively, due to decreased food consumption.

- Using new data, the report reaffirms previously established recommended levels of protein intake, which is 0.8 grams per kilogram of body weight for adults; however, recommended levels for pregnancy are increased.

- The report doesn't set maximum levels for saturated fat, cholesterol, or *trans* fatty acids, as increased risk exists at levels above zero; however, the recommendation is to eat as little as possible while consuming a diet adequate in other important essential nutrients.

- Recommendations are made for linoleic acid (an omega-6 fatty acid) and for alpha-linolenic acid (an omega-3 fatty acid).

Institute of Medicine. Dietary Reference Intakes for Macronutrients Report. September 5, 2002.

How to Understand and Use the Nutrition Facts Label

The FDA developed another set of standards that combines several different sets of guidelines into one standard for a food label called the Daily Value. The **Percent Daily Value** you find on a food label is based on a 2,000 calorie diet. If you are buying food, it is important to know how to read package labels. By knowing how to read the food facts on the food label, you will be able to make wise choices and meet the daily recommendations.

1. The serving size: The first place you should look on the food label is the serving size, and the number of servings in the package. In the sample label of macaroni and cheese (Figure 6-1), if you ate the whole package, you would have eaten two cups and therefore need to multiply the calories and other nutrient amounts by two.

2. Calories (and calories from fat): In this section you will find the number of total calories per serving, as well as the number of calories that come from fat. In the sample label of macaroni and cheese, notice that almost half the calories come from fat.

3. Limit these nutrients: This section lists nutrients that Americans get in adequate or more than adequate amounts and that are associated with diseases. *Trans* fat is a recent addition to this section.

4. Get enough of these: The nutrients listed in this section of the food label are important nutrients for reducing the risk of disease. Most individuals do not get enough of these.

5. Footnote: The footnote defines the percent Daily Values based on a 2,000 calorie diet. It shows the recommended amounts of certain nutrients based on a 2,000 and 2,500 calorie diet.

6. Percent Daily Value (%DV): The %DV are based on the daily value recommendations for key nutrients based on a 2,000 calorie diet. The %DV helps you to determine if a serving of food is high or low in a nutrient (*trans* fat does not have a %DV).

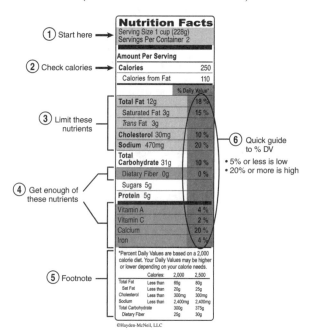

FIGURE 6-1. Nutrition facts.

When reading labels, it is also important to read through the ingredients list. Ingredients are listed in descending order of weight. By looking through the ingredients, you can determine if sugars, fats (especially *trans* fats), and other additives and chemicals have been added to the product. It is useful to compare similar products to find a product that has the most natural and best quality ingredients.

How to Determine a Serving Size

Here are some tips to help you correctly estimate the size of your food portions. You may need to use measuring spoons and cups at first to have an accurate measure.

FOOD SERVING	SERVING SIZE EQUIVALENT
1 teaspoon of margarine/butter	tip of your thumb
1 ounce of cheese	your thumb or four dice stacked together
3 ounces of meat	a deck of cards, the palm of your hand, or an audiocassette tape
½ cup of rice or cooked vegetables	an ice cream scoop
2 tablespoons of peanut butter	a ping-pong ball
1 cup of pasta	a woman's fist or a tennis ball
1 medium potato	a computer mouse
1 apple/peach/orange/pear	a baseball

A Guide to Daily Food Choices

The United States Department of Agriculture (USDA) unveiled the **MyPlate** food guidance system in 2011 to streamline the now obsolete MyPyramid. The new system is meant to simplify healthy eating, providing an online interface that details a variety of helpful dietary information. It also gives users the ability to customize their dietary needs. The new *MyPlate* system and its interactive program found on the ChooseMyPlate site is meant to encourage people to think about what goes on their plate and to become more physically active. Some key tips include the following:

- Make half your plate fruits and vegetables.

- Enjoy your food, but eat less—avoid oversized portions.

- At least half of your grains should be whole grains.

- Drink water instead of sugary drinks.

- Compare the sodium in your foods.

- Switch to fat-free or low-fat (1%) milk

- Eat fewer foods that are high in solid fats.

- Be physically active.

Keep in mind that the amounts of fruits, vegetable, whole grains, proteins and dairy you need vary depending on your age, sex, and level of physical activity. You can find this information on the many charts available for you on the ChooseMyPlate.gov website. As far as what constitutes being physically active, the recommended amount of physical activity for adults aged 18–64 years old is at least 2 hours and 30 minutes each week of aerobic physical activity at a moderate level OR 1 hour and 15 minutes each week of aerobic physical activity at a vigorous level. Being active 5 or more hours each week can provide even more health benefits. Spreading aerobic activity out over at least 3 days a week is best. Also, each activity should be done for at least 10 minutes at a time. Adults should also do strengthening activities, like push-ups, sit-ups and lifting weights, at least 2 days a week. (Ref ChooseMyPlate.gov)

Dietary Guidelines for Americans

In 1980, the U.S. Department of Health and Human Services (HHS) and the U.S. Department of Agriculture (USDA) joined efforts to provide science-based advice for reducing risk of diseases and promoting health through a proper diet and physical activity. These recommendations are called the Dietary Guidelines for Americans and are updated every five years. Below you will find the current recommendations, updated in 2010.

Balancing Calories to Manage Weight

- Prevent and/or reduce overweight and obesity through improved eating and physical activity behaviors.

- Control total calorie intake to manage body weight. For people who are overweight or obese, this will mean consuming fewer calories from foods and beverages.

- Increase physical activity and reduce time spent in sedentary behaviors.

- Maintain appropriate calorie balance during each stage of life—childhood, adolescence, adulthood, pregnancy and breastfeeding, and older age.

Foods and Food Components to Reduce

- Reduce daily sodium intake to less than 2,300 milligrams (mg) and further reduce intake to 1,500 mg among persons who are 51 and older and those of any age who are African American or have hypertension, diabetes, or chronic kidney disease. The 1,500 mg recommendation applies to about half of the U.S. population, including children, and the majority of adults.

> **DID YOU KNOW?**
>
> The average American drinks 526 12-oz. sodas per year... that's 1.5 cans each day. Swap those empty calories for water and you'll cut out over 6,000 calories per month. According to a 2011 study conducted by the Centers for Disease Control and Prevention, the average male consumes 175 calories a day from drinks containing added sugar; females came in at 94 calories. These drinks include sodas, fruit drinks, energy drinks, sports drinks, and sweetened bottled waters.

- Consume less than 10 percent of calories from saturated fatty acids by replacing them with mono-unsaturated and polyunsaturated fatty acids.

- Consume less than 300 mg per day of dietary cholesterol.

- Keep *trans* fatty acid consumption as low as possible by limiting foods that contain synthetic sources of *trans* fats, such as partially hydrogenated oils, and by limiting other solid fats.

- Reduce the intake of calories from solid fats and added sugars.

- Limit the consumption of foods that contain refined grains, especially refined grain foods that contain solid fats, added sugars, and sodium.

- If alcohol is consumed, it should be consumed in moderation—up to one drink per day for women and two drinks per day for men—and only by adults of legal drinking age.

Foods and Nutrients to Increase

Individuals should meet the following recommendations as part of a healthy eating pattern while staying within their calorie needs.

- Increase vegetable and fruit intake.

- Eat a variety of vegetables, especially dark green and red and orange vegetables, and beans and peas.

- Consume at least half of all grains as whole grains. Increase whole-grain intake by replacing refined grains with whole grains.

- Increase intake of fat-free or low-fat milk and milk products, such as milk, yogurt, cheese, or fortified soy beverages.

- Choose a variety of protein foods, which include seafood, lean meat and poultry, eggs, beans and peas, soy products, and unsalted nuts and seeds.

- Increase the amount and variety of seafood consumed by choosing seafood in place of some meat and poultry.

- Replace protein foods that are higher in solid fats with choices that are lower in solid fats and calories and/or are sources of oils.

- Use oils to replace solid fats where possible.

- Choose foods that provide more potassium, dietary fiber, calcium, and vitamin D, which are nutrients of concern in American diets. These foods include vegetables, fruits, whole grains, and milk and milk products.

Building Healthy Eating Patterns

- Select an eating pattern that meets nutrient needs over time at an appropriate calorie level.

- Account for all foods and beverages consumed and assess how they fit within a total healthy eating pattern.

- Follow food safety recommendations when preparing and eating foods to reduce the risk of food-borne illnesses.

Dietary Guidelines for Americans, 2010 (Policy Document) Executive Summary (includes Key Recommendations) http://www.cnpp.usda.gov/DGAs2010-PolicyDocument.htm

Weight Management

The majority of Americans are overweight and obese, and achieving and maintaining a healthy body weight is a big concern. The more important issue is controlling the amount of body fat. An individual is categorized as overweight or obese based on his/her body mass index or BMI.

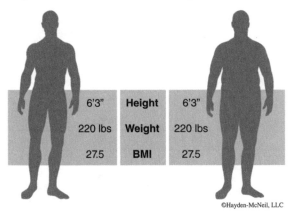

	6'3"	**Height**	6'3"
	220 lbs	**Weight**	220 lbs
	27.5	**BMI**	27.5

©Hayden-McNeil, LLC

Body weight is maintained by consuming the same number of calories you expend each day. An individual's body weight increases when the number of calories consumed over a period of time is consistently greater than the number of calories expended each day. An individual's body weight will decrease when the number of calories consumed over a period of time is consistently less than the number of calories expended each day.

Calorie expenditure can be broken down into three different components: basal metabolic rate (BMR), food digestion, and physical activity. BMR accounts for 55–75% of total energy expenditure (TEE) each day. BMR is the amount of energy required to maintain the function of vital organs at rest. BMR is most affected by muscle mass. Individuals with a higher percentage of muscle mass will have a higher BMR; therefore, males will have a higher BMR than females. As we age, BMR decreases due to decreases in muscle mass. The digestion of food requires energy and makes up 5–15% of TEE. Physical activity is the component that we have the most control over. It accounts for 10–40% of TEE each day. Exercise results in a temporary increase in BMR.

Your BMR can be determined by indirect calorimetry in a laboratory setting by measuring the amount of carbon dioxide you expend. This requires time and money. Handheld devices, a less expensive option, have been developed that measure oxygen consumption. These devices are easier to use and one, the MEDGEM, has been found to be relatively accurate to indirect calorimetry. A free and simple way to determine your BMR is to estimate it. Table 6-6 shows estimates of the amounts of calories needed to maintain calorie balance for various gender and ages based on three different levels of physical activity.

These are only estimates, and estimation of individual calorie needs can be aided with online tools such as those available at ChooseMyPlate.gov. The overall process of losing weight or maintaining weight seems very simple; however, many individuals struggle with maintaining a healthy body weight. Much of this struggle is due to lack of education of what a balanced diet should consist of, how many servings should be consumed from the various food groups, and, most importantly, how much is a serving size. While their weight was gained over a period of time, most individuals want to have a rapid weight loss. As a result of the desire for a quick fix, a number of diets, pills, and surgical procedures have been developed to satisfy the desire of many Americans to lose weight.

Table 6-5. Overweight and Obese: What Do They Mean?

Body weight status can be categorized as underweight, healthy weight, overweight, or obese. Body mass index (BMI) is a useful tool that can be used to estimate an individual's body weight status. BMI is a measure of weight in kilograms (kg) relative to height in meters (m) squared. The terms overweight and obese describe ranges of weight that are greater than what is considered healthy for a given height. These categories are a guide, and some people at a healthy weight also may have weight-responsive health conditions. Because children and adolescents are growing, their BMI is plotted on growth charts[1] for sex and age. The percentile indicates the relative position of the child's BMI among children of the same sex and age.

CATEGORY	CHILDREN AND ADOLESCENTS (BMI FOR AGE PERCENTILE RANGE)	ADULTS (BMI)
Underweight	Less than the 5th percentile	Less than 18.5 kg/m^2
Healthy weight	5th percentile to less than the 85th percentile	18.5 to 24.9 kg/m^2
Overweight	85th percentile to less than the 95th percentile	25.0 to 29.9 kg/m^2
Obese	Equal to or greater than the 95th percentile	30.0 kg/m^2 or greater

Adult BMI can be calculated at http://www.nhlbi.nih.gov/guidelines/obesity/BMI/bmicalc.htm. A child and adolescent BMI calculator is available at http://apps.nccd.cdc.gov/dnpabmi/.

[1] Growth charts are available at http://www.cdc.gov/growthcharts.

Source: U.S. Department of Agriculture

Table 6-6. Estimated Calorie Needs per Day by Age, Gender, and Physical Activity Level[a]

Estimated amounts of calories needed to maintain calorie balance for various gender and age groups at three different levels of physical activity. The estimates are rounded to the nearest 200 calories. An individual's calorie needs may be higher or lower than these average estimates.

| GENDER | AGE (YEARS) | PHYSICAL ACTIVITY LEVEL[b] | | |
		SEDENTARY	MODERATELY ACTIVE	ACTIVE
Child (female and male)	2–3	1,000–1,200[c]	1,000–1,400[c]	1,000–1,400[c]
Female[d]	4–8	1,200–1,400	1,400–1,600	1,400–1,800
	9–13	1,400–1,600	1,600–2,000	1,800–2,200
	14–18	1,800	2,000	2,400
	19–30	1,800–2,000	2,000–2,200	2,400
	31–50	1,800	2,000	2,200
	51+	1,600	1,800	2,000–2,200
Male	4–8	1,200–1,400	1,400–1,600	1,600–2,000
	9–13	1,600–2,000	1,800–2,200	2,000–2,600
	14–18	2,000–2,400	2,400–2,800	2,800–3,200
	19–30	2,400–2,600	2,600–2,800	3,000
	31–50	2,200–2,400	2,400–2,600	2,800–3,000
	51+	2,000–2,200	2,200–2,400	2,400–2,800

a. Based on Estimated Energy Requirements (EER) equations, using reference heights (average) and reference weights (healthy) for each age/gender group. For children and adolescents, reference height and weight vary. For adults, the reference man is 5 feet 10 inches tall and weighs 154 pounds. The reference woman is 5 feet 4 inches tall and weighs 126 pounds. EER equations are from the Institute of Medicine. Dietary Reference Intakes for Energy, Carbohydrate, Fiber, Fat, Fatty Acids, Cholesterol, Protein, and Amino Acids. Washington (DC): The National Academies Press; 2002.

b. Sedentary means a lifestyle that includes only the light physical activity associated with typical day-to-day life. Moderately active means a lifestyle that includes physical activity equivalent to walking about 1.5 to 3 miles per day at 3 to 4 miles per hour, in addition to the light physical activity associated with typical day-to-day life. Active means a lifestyle that includes physical activity equivalent to walking more than 3 miles per day at 3 to 4 miles per hour, in addition to the light physical activity associated with typical day-to-day life.

c. The calorie ranges shown are to accommodate needs of different ages within the group. For children and adolescents, more calories are needed at older ages. For adults, fewer calories are needed at older ages.

d. Estimates for females do not include women who are pregnant or breastfeeding.

Source: U.S. Department of Agriculture

Overall, many popular diets are based on a negative energy balance, meaning you consume fewer calories than you expend. An individual can experience rapid weight loss with the diets currently available; however, the majority of this rapid weight that is lost is due to water weight loss. As a result of the restrictive nature of the diet, or high consumption of certain foods, many individuals are unable to sustain the diet and return to their old habits. Since they were not properly educated, when individuals return to their normal diet habits after experimenting with a new diet, the result is gaining back the weight lost and perhaps even more. This is termed **weight cycling**, especially if the individual attempts many diets.

A balance must be attained between calories ingested and calories burned to maintain healthy weight. Table 6-6 provides you with estimates for your daily calorie needs. It is also handy for you to know how many calories you burn for different physical activities so you can monitor how you are balancing your needs with your expenditure. There are many different calorie expenditure applications to be found on the web. For instance ChooseMyPlate.gov provides you with the **SuperTracker,** which helps you plan, analyze, and track your diet and physical activity. Table 6-7 is an example of a calorie burn equation that includes several different activities. Every activity you do burns calories. By lowering your calorie intake and increasing your activity, you will create a calorie deficit that should result in weight loss. Keep in mind, men burn calories faster than women and heavier people burn calories faster than thin people. Exactly how many calories are expended by any individual will vary.

Table 6-7 gives the approximate number of calories burned per minute of a variety of activities. For each activity, multiply your exact weight by the number in the per pound column to equal the number of calories burned per minute. Multiply this number by the number of minutes in that activity to equal total calories burned.

If changing one's body composition is your goal, try changing your ratio between lean body mass and fat mass. Focusing solely on weight loss without some type of resistance training to increase lean body mass will be a less effective strategy. When monitoring weight loss, keep in mind that slow and steady weight loss stays off, but quick weight loss reappears! A reasonable target is 0.5–1 pound per week for someone who weighs less than 150 pounds and 1 to 2 pounds for someone heavier. There are 3500 calories in one pound of fat, so a recommendation

would be to create an imbalance for the week by dividing 3500 calories by 7 (days of the week) which would give you 500 calories a day for you to burn through activity, reduce through your diet, or an even better plan would be to do both at 250 calories each. This should put you at a 1-pound deficit at the end of a seven-day period. You should watch your portion sizes and never skip meals. The food you eat fuels your metabolism, which is your internal energy source. If you feed your metabolism with several small meals throughout the day you will help sustain a constant energy source for your body to burn the foods you are eating. If you skip a meal, you can slow your metabolism down and lower your amount of energy, creating a tired feeling.

Some individuals may have the sole desire to gain lean body mass as opposed to any type of weight loss. Again, this involves a relationship between caloric intake and energy expenditure. In theory, for weight gain, you need to consume 500 calories above your typical intake every day to gain 1 pound a week. Weight gain can be achieved by increasing the size of your muscle mass as well as by including muscle-building resistance exercises into your workouts. If you choose to increase your calorie intake, you can do that by eating a larger volume of food or by choosing foods that are energy-dense (high in calories). Either way, you should choose foods that are nutrient-dense instead of settling for high-calorie junk foods. Nutrient-dense foods include fruits, vegetables, and whole grains. Foods that are both energy- and nutrient-dense include legumes, nuts, seeds, olives, and avocados. You may also want to increase your consumption of dairy products, meats, seafood and poultry. Use seasoning blends, herbs, and spices to add flavor and aroma. The main goal is to increase your overall intake of calories every day either by eating more meals or by increasing the size of the meals you eat. Your meals should be balanced with the right amounts of protein, carbohydrates, and fat. Follow MyPlate guidelines when filling your plate with a protein source such as meat, poultry, fish, seafood, legumes, or tofu and serve it with a side of green and colorful vegetables. Add a serving of starchy foods such as potatoes, sweet corn, rice or pasta as energy-dense carbohydrate sources. If you prefer to snack on smaller meals throughout the day, choose energy-dense foods, such as trail mix made with dried fruit, nuts and seeds. You can eat sandwiches made with peanut or other nut butters, or use meats and add calories with slices of cheese or avocado.

Individuals who are confused about all the information obtained through the media should speak with a licensed dietician and develop a nutrition and exercise plan that is appropriate for them. A number of studies have shown that following a well-balanced diet, as described in this chapter, and expending energy through regular physical activity, is the best way to lose and maintain a healthy body weight.

Table 6-7. Calorie Burn Equation

EXAMPLE:

Calories burned per pound per minute (badminton – .044) × (times) your exact weight (140 pounds) = (equals) total calories burned per minute (6.16 calories burned per minute) × (times) minutes of activity (30 minutes) = (equals) 184.80 total calories burned per activity

ACTIVITY (ALPHABETICAL)	CALORIES BURNED PER POUND PER MINUTE	YOUR EXACT WEIGHT IN POUNDS	TOTAL CALORIES BURNED PER MINUTE	MINUTES OF ACTIVITY	TOTAL CALORIES BURNED
Badminton	.044				
Basketball	.063				
Bicycling (5.5 mph)	.029				
Bicycling (9.5 mph)	.045				
Climbing hills (no load)	.055				
Dancing, ballroom	.023				
Dance, Aerobic, medium	.046				
Dance, Aerobic, intense	.061				
Golf	.038				
Jumping rope (70 jumps per minute)	.074				
Mowing the lawn	.051				
Racquetball	.081				
Running (6-minute mile)	.115				
Running (8-minute mile)	.095				
Running (9-minute mile)	.087				
Swimming, crawl, slow	.058				
Swimming, breast stroke, fast	.074				
Walking, normal pace, asphalt road	.036				
Walking, normal pace, fields and hills	.037				
Weight training, free weights	.039				
Weight training, circuit training	.042				
Volleyball	.023				

Source: http://whatscookingamerica.net/Information/CalorieBurnChart.htm

Summary Questions

1. What is the least healthy food you eat every day? Identify at least one substitute that would be healthier but just as satisfying.

2. What factors influence your food choices (e.g., convenience, cost, availability, habit)?

3. Based on what you have read, a good diet consists of eating the "right" kinds of carbohydrates and the "right" kinds of fat. Which do you consider the "right" carbohydrates and the "right" fat in your diet?

4. What is the leading source of added sugars in the American diet today?

References

Books

Brand-Miller, J.; Wolever, T.; Foster-Powell, K.; & Colagiuri, S. (2002). *The New Glucose Revolution*. Marlow & Company.

Clark, N. (2008). *Nancy Clark Sports Nutrition Guidebook*, 4th edition. Champaign, IL: Human Kinetics.

Drewnowski, A. Ph.D. (2007). The Rising Cost of Low-Energy-Density Foods. *Journal of the American Dietetic Association*, 107(12): 2071–2076.

Fahey, T.D.; Insel, P.M.; & Roth, W.T. (2001). *Fit & Well*, 4th edition. Mountain View, CA: Mayfield Publishing Company.

Gershoff, S. (1990). *The Tufts University Guide to Total Nutrition*. New York, NY: Harper and Row Publishers.

Maughan, R.J. & Burke, L.M. (2002). *Sports Nutrition*. Malden, MA: Blackwell Science Ltd.

Mayers, J. (1990). *Diet and Nutrition Guide*. New York, NY: Scripps Howard Company.

Mozaffarian, D. M.D., Ph.D.; Hao, T. M.P.H.; Rimm, E.B. Sc.D.; Willett, W.C. M.D., Ph.D.; & Hu, F.B. M.D., Ph.D. (2011). Changes in Diet and Lifestyle and Long-Term Weight Gain in Men and Women. *New England Journal of Medicine*, 364: 2392–404.

Netzer, C.T. (1994). *The Complete Book of Food Counts*. New York, NY: Dell Publishing.

Ogden, C.L.; Kit, B.K.; Carroll, M.D.; & Park, S. (2011). Consumption of sugar drinks in the United States, 2005–2008. *National Center for Health Statistics* data brief, no 71. Hyattsville, MD: National Center for Health Statistics.

Pritikin, R. (1999). *The Pritikin Weight Loss Breakthrough*. New York, NY: Signet Books.

Thompson, J. & Manore, M. (2005). *Nutrition: An Applied Approach*. San Francisco: Benjamin Cummings.

Van Horn, L. (2011). Calories Count: But Can Consumers Count on Them? *The Journal of the American Medical Association*, 306(3):315–316.

Wardlaw, G.M.; Insel, P.M.; & Seyler, M.F. (1994). *Contemporary Nutrition Issues and Insights*. St. Louis, MO: Mosby-Year Book, Inc.

Wildman, R. & Miller, B. (2004). *Sports and Fitness Nutrition*. Belmont, CA: Wadsworth/Thompson Learning.

Newsletters

"Harvard Women's Health Watch." Harvard Medical School Health Publications Group, 164 Longwood Avenue, Boston, MA 02115. E-mail HWH@Warren.Med.Harvard.Edu.

"Nutrition Action Health Letter." Center for Science in the Public Interest, Suite 300, 1875 Connecticut Avenue, NW, Washington, DC 20009-5728.

"Tufts University Diet and Nutrition Letter." Tufts Diet and Nutrition Letter. P.O. Box 57857, Boulder, CO 80322-7857. Customer Service: 1-800-274-7581.

"University of California at Berkeley Wellness Letter." Health Letter, P.O. Box 420148, Palm Coast, FL 32142. Telephone: (904) 445-6414.

Government Publications

U.S. Department of Agriculture
Human Nutrition Information Service
Nutrition Education Division
Belcrest Road
Hyattsville, MD 20782
Telephone: (301) 436-5724

Institute of Medicine. *Dietary Reference Intakes for Macronutrients Report*. September 5, 2002.

Web Sites

http://www.ChooseMyPlate.gov
Nutrition and exercise information includes food and physical activity trackers

http://www.heart.org/HEARTORG/GettingHealthy/
FatsAndOils/Fats101/My-Fats-Translator_
UCM_428869_Article.jsp#.T1u23DEgeDQ
Calorie requirement calculator

http://www.mayoclinic.com/health/trans-fat/CL00032
Trans *fat information*

http://www.cnpp.usda.gov/dgas2010-policydocument.
htm
Dietary Guidelines

http://ods.od.nih.gov/factsheets/dietarysupplements/
Dietary Supplements

http://www.thehealthyeatingguide.com/
healthyeatingstatistics.html
Healthy Eating Guide

MyPyramid Worksheet

Check how you did today and set a goal to aim for tomorrow

MyPyramid.gov
STEPS TO A HEALTHIER YOU

Food Group	Tip	Goal Based on a 2000 calorie pattern.	List each food choice in its food group*	Write in Your Choices for Today	Estimate Your Total
GRAINS	Make at least half your grains whole grains	**6 ounce equivalents** (1 ounce equivalent is about 1 slice bread, 1 cup dry cereal, or ½ cup cooked rice, pasta, or cereal)			ounce equivalents
VEGETABLES	Try to have vegetables from several subgroups each day	**2 ½ cups** Subgroups: Dark Green, Orange, Starchy, Dry Beans and Peas, Other Veggies			cups
FRUITS	Make most choices fruit, not juice	**2 cups**			cups
MILK	Choose fat-free or low fat most often	**3 cups** (1 ½ ounces cheese = 1 cup milk)			cups
MEAT & BEANS	Choose lean meat and poultry. Vary your choices—more fish, beans, peas, nuts, and seeds	**5 ½ ounce equivalents** (1 ounce equivalent is 1 ounce meat, poultry, or fish, 1 egg, 1 T. peanut butter, ½ ounce nuts, or ¼ cup dry beans)			ounce equivalents
PHYSICAL ACTIVITY	Build more physical activity into your daily routine at home and work.	At least **30 minutes** of moderate to vigorous activity a day, 10 minutes or more at a time.	*Some foods don't fit into any group. These "extras" may be mainly fat or sugar— limit your intake of these.		minutes

How did you do today? ☐ Great   ☐ So-So   ☐ Not so Great

My food goal for tomorrow is: _____

My activity goal for tomorrow is: _____

chapter 7

Wellness
Cardiovascular Health

by Keith Howard, M.A.

Cardiovascular disease is a disease of the heart and blood vessels. It is considered one of the leading causes of death in the United States. The major form of cardiovascular disease is coronary heart disease (CHD). In **coronary heart disease**, the arteries supplying the heart with oxygen and nutrients become lined with fatty deposits that build up over a period of time and restrict the capability of the system to work to its fullest potential. Severe blockage may result in a heart attack or stroke. Approximately 1.5 million heart attacks occur each year, and 500,000 result in death.

Risk Factors for Coronary Heart Disease (CHD)

The American Heart Association (AHA) suggests that risk factors for CHD are grouped into two categories: primary, or major risk factors, and secondary, or contributing risk factors. Primary risk factors have been found to have a direct relationship to coronary heart disease while secondary risk factors contribute to CHD, but their exact contribution has yet to be determined. Additionally, some of these risk factors can be modified, controlled, or treated, while some cannot.

Uncontrollable Primary Risk Factors

The three primary risk factors that are out of the control of the individual are age, sex, and genetics (heredity).

Age

The risk of developing coronary heart disease is greater as one gets older. Half of heart attacks occur in people 65 or older. This is due to the fact that plaque (fatty deposits) has had more years to collect on the arterial walls. In addition, as people age, they may have a tendency to exercise less and under-utilize the cardiovascular system.

7
___
Chapter
Seven

Sex (Gender)

Men, as compared to women, are more likely to develop coronary heart disease before age 40. Before age 40, it is thought that estrogen protects a woman against CHD. An alarming trend is the increased incidence of heart attacks in pre-menopausal women who have been smoking long enough for it to affect their health, especially when combined with oral contraceptive use.

Genetic (Heredity)

One risk is a history of first-degree male relatives (father, grandfather, or brothers) who have had coronary heart disease or who died of coronary heart disease before the age of 55. Also, first-degree female relatives (mother, grandmother, or sisters) who have had coronary heart disease or who died of coronary heart disease before the age of 65 indicates a strong familial tendency. These people are strongly encouraged to keep the other risk factors as low as possible.

Controllable Primary Risk Factors

There are several primary factors that can indicate the likelihood that an individual will develop some form of heart disease which involve conditions or behaviors that can be controlled and treated via lifestyle modifications and/or medication.

Cigarette Smoking

Medical professionals consider cigarette smoking the most harmful of the preventable risk factors associated with chronic illness and premature death. Cigarette smoking is responsible for one of every five deaths annually in the United States. It contributes to approximately 430,000 premature deaths from cardiovascular and pulmonary diseases, not to mention cancer-related deaths. Smoking increases heart rate and blood pressure while restricting blood flow, making it easier for fatty deposits to form on arterial walls and increasing the chance that blockage may occur.

High Cholesterol

The risk of coronary heart disease increases as cholesterol levels increase. **Cholesterol** is a fatty, wax-like substance that circulates through the bloodstream and is necessary for proper functioning of the body. Our bodies obtain cholesterol in two ways: from the liver, which manufactures it, and from the foods we eat. Cholesterol levels vary depending on diet, age, gender, heredity, and other factors.

Cholesterol is carried in protein-lipid packages called lipoproteins. **Low density lipoproteins (LDL)** shuttle cholesterol from the liver to the organs that require it. LDL is known as "bad" cholesterol because if there is more than the body can use, the excess is deposited in the blood vessels. When it accumulates, it can block arteries and cause heart attacks and strokes. **High density lipoproteins (HDL)**, or "good" cholesterol, shuttle unused cholesterol back to the liver for recycling. Those with a cholesterol level below 200 mg/dl are considered at low risk for developing CHD. High LDL levels and low HDL levels are associated with a high risk for CHD. HDL is especially important because a high HDL level seems to offer protection from CHD even in cases where total cholesterol is high. The ratio of total cholesterol to high-density lipoproteins is considered one of the best indicators predicting cardiovascular disease.

High Blood Pressure

Hypertension, or high blood pressure, occurs when too much force or pressure is exerted against the wall of the arteries. If your blood pressure is high, your heart has to work harder to push the blood throughout your system. Over time, a strained and over-taxed heart may weaken and enlarge. Increased blood pressure may also scar and harden arteries. Generally, a systolic blood pressure over 140 mmHg or a diastolic pressure over 90 mmHg is considered high. Keys to controlling blood pressure are regular aerobic exercise, weight control, smoking cessation, and a low-fat and low-salt diet.

Physical Inactivity

The American Heart Association has officially recognized physical inactivity as a major risk factor for cardiovascular disease. An estimated 35 to 50 million Americans are sedentary, increasing their risk for developing CHD. Exercise is thought to be the closest thing to a "magic bullet" against heart disease. Research suggests that regular vigorous aerobic exercise 3 to 4 times a week not only decreases a person's chance of developing CHD, but also improves a person's chance of survival if they have a heart attack. Aerobic exercise can also help negate other primary and secondary risk factors such as high cholesterol, high blood pressure, obesity, diabetes, and stress.

Obesity

Obese individuals make up over 30% of the American adult population. Individuals are considered obese if they have a body mass index (BMI) over 30, or over 24% body fat in males and over 28% body fat in females. Due to excess body weight and fat, a greater strain is placed on the heart. In general, most obese individuals are not active, therefore they are more susceptible to problems associated with other risk factors such as high blood pressure, high cholesterol, and diabetes. For those who are obese, losing even a small amount, such as 10%, of their body weight can have very beneficial effects on cardiovascular health, including a reduction in blood pressure.

Diabetes

Diabetes is a disease characterized by high blood sugar (glucose) levels. Over 80% of diabetics die from some form of cardiovascular disease. This may be due to the fact that most diabetics have trouble metabolizing fat, which may lead to an increased buildup of fatty deposits on the linings of the arterial walls. A person can help control the risk associated with diabetes by increasing physical activity and monitoring diet. In Type 1 diabetes, no insulin is produced, and so it must be injected daily. Type 1 diabetes occurs early in life. Type 2 diabetes occurs most often in middle-aged, overweight, sedentary adults, as well as overweight, sedentary youth. Excessive weight is a factor because it increases cellular resistance to insulin. In contrast, exercise decreases insulin resistance. Type 2 diabetes makes up approximately 90% of all individuals diagnosed with diabetes. Data indicate that at least 75% of new cases of type 2 diabetes can be prevented through regular exercise and maintaining normal weight. Diabetes has numerous long-range complications, which primarily involve degenerative disorders of the blood vessels and nerves.

Secondary Risk Factors

Stress

Excessive stress can increase a person's chance of developing CHD. Chronic stress places a constant strain on the cardiovascular system, which can lead to CHD. Stress increases both the cholesterol in the blood as well as blood pressure. Individuals under excessive stress tend to be smokers, overeat, and exercise less often. Generally, Type A personalities (high-achievers who are hurried, competitive, and angry) tend to have a higher incidence of coronary heart disease.

Alcohol Consumption

Individuals that consume excessive levels of alcohol on a regular basis increase the development of health issues relating to, but not limited to, cardiovascular heart disease (CHD). Alcohol consumption is positively correlated to an increase in blood pressure and can even lead to stroke or heart failure. To reduce the probability of developing alcohol-related cardiovascular issues an individual should keep consumption at a moderate level or below. For males, it is recommended to consume no more than two drinks per day while females should consume only one drink per day. An average alcoholic beverage is measured to be roughly one 12 oz. beer, a 4 oz. glass of wine, or 1.5 oz. of liquor spirits. Individuals that do not drink alcohol are not encouraged to do so since other health issues outside the scope of cardiovascular disease may develop as a result.

Diet and Nutrition

An individual's diet can have a significant positive impact on several factors relating to cardiovascular health. Choosing the right foods on a regular basis can help exert control over some of the primary risk factors of cardiovascular heart disease. A proper diet will reduce cholesterol levels, lower blood pressure, help maintain a healthy weight, and help manage issues relating to diabetes. Additionally, by combining the appropriate frequency and intensity levels of physical activity with good nutritional eating habits, individuals can positively impact their health by both controlling the impact of risk factors and by minimizing the likelihood of developing the risk factors of CHD.

Evaluating, Managing, and Preventing Cardiovascular Heart Disease

After examining the primary and secondary risk factors, there are certain lifestyle changes that, if adopted, can help prevent future coronary heart disease. These lifestyle changes include the following:

- Do not smoke.

- Adopt or follow a low-fat and low-salt diet.

- Maintain an appropriate body weight.

- Exercise on a regular basis.

- Learn to cope and manage stress (see Chapter 8).

- Have a yearly physical examination by a well-trained physician.

Smoking

If you're ready, *Clearing the Air: A Guide to Quitting Smoking*, available from the American Cancer Society, offers these recommendations for quitting smoking:

1. Identify reasons for quitting.
2. Set a target date for quitting.
3. Identify your barriers to quitting.
4. Make specific plans ahead of time for dealing with temptations.
5. Change to a brand you find distasteful.
6. Involve friends and family.
7. On the day you quit, toss out all cigarettes and matches.
8. After you quit, change your normal routine and location associated with smoking.
9. When you get the "crazies," chew gum, carrots, sunflower seeds, etc.
10. Mark progress; celebrate anniversaries.

Diet

1. Consume less than 10% of calories from saturated fatty acids, less than 300 mg/day of cholesterol, and keep *trans* fatty acid consumption as low as possible.

2. Keep total fat intake between 20–35% of calories, with most fats coming from sources of polyunsaturated and monounsaturated fatty acids, such as fish, nuts, and vegetable oils.

3. Switch to skim milk rather than 2% or whole.

4. Eat less fried food.

5. Avoid foods that include sauces, gravies, or oily dressings.

6. Trim all visible fats from meats before and after cooking.

7. Don't eat the skin from poultry; it contains fat and cholesterol.

8. Choose to eat a meatless dish one or two meals per week.

9. Choose low-fat snacks such as fresh fruits, raw vegetables, or salt-free pretzels rather than fatty chips, cookies, etc.

10. Eat fish twice a week; baked or broiled, not fried.

Physical Activity

Participate in regular physical activity and reduce sedentary activities to promote health, psychological well-being, and a healthy body weight.

- To reduce the risk of chronic disease in adulthood, participate in at least 30 minutes of moderate-intensity physical activity, above usual activity, at work or home on most days of the week.

- For most people, greater health benefits can be obtained by engaging in physical activity of more vigorous intensity or longer duration.

- To help manage body weight and prevent gradual, unhealthy body weight gain in adulthood, participate in approximately 60 minutes of moderate-to-vigorous activity on most days of the week while not exceeding caloric intake requirements.

- To sustain weight loss in adulthood, engage in at least 60 to 90 minutes of daily moderate-intensity physical activity while not exceeding caloric intake requirements. Some people may need to consult with a healthcare provider before participating in this level of activity.

Physical Examination

A regular physical examination by your physician can help prevent the development of health-related issues such as cardiovascular heart disease. Regular physical exams are a great way to monitor some of the "unseen" primary risk factors such as high cholesterol levels and high blood pressure. Everyone should be aware of their total serum cholesterol. If your cholesterol levels are found to be heading in the wrong direction ask your doctor if dietary modifications and/or increased physical activity are recommended when making a regular office visit. You may refer to the following tables for some of the guidelines dealing with cholesterol levels and blood pressure ranges in order to determine your risk of developing cardiovascular disease.

Cholesterol Guidelines

Table 7-1. Risk Profile—Lipid and Lipoprotein Concentrations

TOTAL CHOLESTEROL	RISK
<200 mg/dl	Desirable
200 to 239 mg/dl	Borderline
>240 mg/dl	High
LDL CHOLESTEROL	RISK
<100 mg/dl	Optimal
100 to 129 mg/dl	Near optimal/above optimal
130 to 159 mg/dl	Borderline high
160 to 189 mg/dl	High
>190 mg/dl	Very high
HDL CHOLESTEROL	RISK
40 mg/dl	Increased risk
60 mg/dl	Heart protective
TRIGLYCERIDES	RISK
150 mg/dl	Normal
150 to 199 mg/dl	Borderline high
200 to 499 mg/dl	High
>500 mg/dl	Very high

Adapted from "Revised Cholesterol Guidelines," July 2001, Harvard Heart Letter.

Blood Pressure

Table 7-2. Classification of Blood Pressure for Adults Age 18 Years and Older

CATEGORY	SYSTOLIC (mmHg)	DIASTOLIC (mmHg)
Optimal	120 to 129	80 to 84
High normal	130 to 139	85 to 89
Hypertension		
Stage 1 (mild)	140 to 159	90 to 99
Stage 2 (moderate)	160 to 179	100 to 109
Stage 3 (severe)	180 to 209	110 to 119
Stage 4 (very severe)	>210	>120

Summary Questions

1. What are the primary and secondary risk factors for coronary heart disease (CHD)? What risk factors can you control?

2. Do you or your immediate family members suffer from any medical conditions such as high blood pressure, high cholesterol, or diabetes? If so, what are you doing to prevent or minimize the impact of these health issues in your life?

3. How would you rate your current eating habits? Are there any types of foods you could add or delete to reduce your risk of developing cardiovascular disease?

4. What role does physical activity play in the prevention of coronary heart disease (CHD)?

5. How much physical activity do you get on a daily basis? Do you feel that the activity you engage in is at a moderate level of intensity or higher?

References

ACSM's Guidelines for Exercise Testing and Prescription. (2004). Seventh Edition, Philadelphia, PA. American Heart Association (1998). *Risk Factors and Coronary Heart Disease. AHA Scientific Position.* Dallas, TX: American Heart Association.

Aspaugh, D.; Hamrick, M.; & Rosato, F. (2003). *Wellness: Concepts and Applications.* First Edition. New York, NY: McGraw-Hill Higher Education.

Donatelle, R.; Snow-Harter, C.; & Wilcox, A. (1995). *Wellness: Choices for Health and Fitness.* Redwood City, CA: Benjamin/Cummings Publishing Co.

Fahey, T.; Insel, P.; & Roth, W. (2001). *Fit and Well.* Mountain View, CA: Mayfield Publishing Company.

Greenberg, J.; Dintiaman, G.; & Myers-Oakes, B. (1995). *Physical Fitness and Wellness.* Needham Heights, MA: Allyn and Bacon.

Hockey, R.V. (1996). *Physical Fitness: The Pathways to Healthful Living.* St. Louis, MO: Mosby-Year Book, Inc.

Hoeger, W. & Hoeger, S. (1999). *Fitness and Wellness.* Englewood, CO: Morton Publishing Co.

Powers, S. (2001). *Exercise Physiology: Theory and Application to Fitness and Performance.* Fourth Edition, New York, NY: McGraw-Hill.

Powers, S. & Dodd, S. (2003). *Total Fitness and Wellness,* Brief Edition. Pearson Education, Inc., published as Benjamin Cummings, San Francisco.

Powers, S. & Dodd, S. (1996). *Total Fitness: Exercise, Nutrition, and Wellness.* Needham Heights, MA: Allyn and Bacon.

Prentice, W. (1999). *Fitness and Wellness for Life.* Boston, MA: WCB/McGraw-Hill.

Robbins, G.; Powers, D.; & Burgess, S. (2002). *A Wellness Way of Life.* Fifth Edition, New York, NY: McGraw-Hill Higher Education.

Seiger, L.; Vanderpool, K.; & Barnes, D. (1995). *Fitness and Wellness Strategies.* Dubuque, IA: William C. Brown Communications, Inc.

Web Sites

http://cardiosmart.org/
American College of Cardiology

https://www.heart360.org/Default.aspx
American Heart Association

http://www.cdc.gov/heartdisease/
Center for Disease Control

http://www.ncbi.nlm.nih.gov/pubmedhealth/
PMH0004449/
PubMed Health

http://www.webmd.com/heart-disease/default.htm
WebMD

chapter 8

Wellness
Stress Management

by Peter Koutroumpis, M.Ed.

What Is Stress?

The term stress is complicated to define. For **stress** to occur, there must be a stimulus, followed by a physiological reaction to that stimulus, and finally a resulting strain. For example, the stimulus, or **stressor**, could be an upcoming exam. This stressor may trigger a reaction such as muscle tension and increased blood pressure. Ultimately, this physiological reaction may result in a headache or feelings of anxiety.

Stress is inevitable. Stress is needed to perform daily tasks of life, and more importantly, to stimulate growth and development. Stress can be beneficial. However, too much stress, especially when it exists for a prolonged period of time and is unrelieved, can result in physical and mental illness.

Dr. Hans Selye, biologist and endocrinologist, defined stress as the "nonspecific response of the body to any demand made upon it." He further pointed out that stress is caused or triggered by stressors that may be physical, social, or psychological and that may be negative or positive in nature.

Selye called human reactions to positive stressors **eustress**, that is, stress that is beneficial, and he used the term **distress** to describe detrimental responses to negative stressors. Often there is a fine line between whether something produces eustress or distress. For example, moderate physical exercise is a stressor that can make you feel better and more fit. However, if you do too much too soon, it can produce distress in the form of soreness or injury.

Sometimes the difference between eustress and distress is a matter of perception; do you perceive the stressor as a threat or a challenge? Although we may habitually respond in ways that seem automatic and beyond our control, we can choose to examine the way we think and then work on changing counterproductive thinking or beliefs.

8

Chapter
Eight

Stress should not be considered solely as a physiological phenomenon. Stress can also be viewed from a psychological or cognitive perspective. Current research suggests that the stress response is not a simple biological response to nonspecific stressors but is instead an interrelated process that includes the presence of a stressor, the circumstances in which the stressor occurs, the interpretation of the situation by the person, his or her typical reaction, and the resources available to deal with the stressor. For example, one person may find downhill skiing fun and exciting, and look forward to taking winter vacations to ski the slopes. Another person may have tried to ski, but because of dislike of cold weather and fear of injury, finds skiing a distressing activity. Therefore the stress response in a given situation is dependent upon the individual's perceptions.

Psychological or Cognitive Response to Stress

Once the stress process is stimulated by the presence of a stressor, psychological or cognitive processes take over, determining the manner in which the stressor is perceived. An individual's perception of a particular situation can elicit a response that may vary from arousal to anxiety. Arousal is the body's heightened awareness that a stressor is present and is a signal to higher centers in the brain to respond (physiological). **Anxiety**, on the other hand, is described by Speilberger as feelings of tension, apprehension, nervousness, and worry. He maintains that these are cognitive rather than biological responses.

The degree to which a particular situation elicits an emotional response depends to a great extent on how the individual appraises the situation and how well prepared he or she feels to handle it. Those individuals who are prone to stress tend to make extreme, absolute, global judgments and engage in cognitive distortions in which they overemphasize the most negative aspects of a given situation. Our thought processes seem automatic, but we need to emphasize the necessity of examining our beliefs and working on changing them when they are erroneous or counterproductive.

Certainly there are both biological and cognitive responses to stressors. Even though we talk about them as two separate processes, they are interrelated and often occur simultaneously.

Physiological Response to Stress

The General Adaptation Syndrome

The **General Adaptation Syndrome** is a sequenced physiological response to the presence of a stressor: the alarm, resistance, recovery, and exhaustion stages of a stress response.

The Alarm Stage

(*also known as the* **fight-or-flight response**)

Once exposed to any event that is seen as threatening, the body immediately prepares for difficulty. Involuntary changes are controlled by hormonal and nervous system functions that quickly prepare the body for the fight-or-flight response. During this stage, the sympathetic nervous system, which is regulated by the hypothalamus, causes the body to do the following:

- Increase heart rate

- Increase force with which heart contracts

- Dilate coronary arteries

- Constrict abdominal arteries

- Dilate pupils

- Dilate bronchial tubes

- Increase strength of skeletal muscles

- Release glucose from liver

- Increase mental activity

- Significantly increase basal metabolic rate

The Resistance Stage

The second stage of response to a stressor, the resistance stage, reflects the body's attempt to reestablish internal balance, or a state of homeostasis. The high level of energy seen in the initial alarm stage cannot be maintained very long. The body therefore attempts to reduce the intensity of the initial response to a more manageable level. This is accomplished by reducing the production of adrenocorticotropic hormone (ACTH), thus allowing specificity of adaptation to occur. Specific organ systems become the focus of the body's response, such as the cardiovascular and digestive systems.

The Recovery Stage

Because of the ability to move from an alarm stage into a less damaging resistance stage, effective coping or a change in the status of the stressor will probably occur. In fact, as control over the stressful situation is gained, homeostasis is even more completely established and movement toward full recovery is seen. At the completion of the recovery stage, the body has returned to its pre-stressed state and there is minimal evidence of the stressor's existence.

The Exhaustion Stage

Body adjustments made as a result of long-term exposure to a stressor often result in an overload. Specific organs and body systems that were called on during the resistance stage may not be able to resist a stressor indefinitely. This results in exhaustion, and the stress-producing hormone levels rise again. In extreme or chronic cases, exhaustion can become so pronounced that death can occur.

The following table will help identify some of the physiological changes that take place in the body during stress. Indicate how often each of the physical symptoms happen to you and then total the points to determine your level of physiological reactivity to stress.

Table 8-1. Physiological Reactions to Stress

Circle the number that best represents the frequency of occurrence of the following physical symptoms and add up the total number of points.

SYMPTOM	NEVER	INFREQUENTLY (more than once in six months)	OCCASIONALLY (more than once per month)	VERY OFTEN (more than once per week)	CONSTANTLY
1. Tension headaches	1	2	3	4	5
2. Migraine (vascular) headaches	1	2	3	4	5
3. Stomach aches	1	2	3	4	5
4. Increase in blood pressure	1	2	3	4	5
5. Cold hands	1	2	3	4	5
6. Acidic stomach	1	2	3	4	5
7. Shallow, rapid breathing	1	2	3	4	5
8. Diarrhea	1	2	3	4	5
9. Palpitations	1	2	3	4	5
10. Shaky hands	1	2	3	4	5
11. Burping	1	2	3	4	5
12. Gassiness	1	2	3	4	5
13. Increased urge to urinate	1	2	3	4	5
14. Sweaty feet/hands	1	2	3	4	5
15. Oily skin	1	2	3	4	5
16. Fatigue/exhausted feeling	1	2	3	4	5
17. Panting	1	2	3	4	5
18. Dry mouth	1	2	3	4	5
19. Hand tremor	1	2	3	4	5
20. Backache	1	2	3	4	5
21. Neck stiffness	1	2	3	4	5
22. Gum chewing	1	2	3	4	5
23. Grinding teeth	1	2	3	4	5
24. Constipation	1	2	3	4	5
25. Tightness in chest or heart	1	2	3	4	5
26. Dizziness	1	2	3	4	5
27. Nausea/vomiting	1	2	3	4	5
28. Menstrual distress	1	2	3	4	5
29. Skin blemishes	1	2	3	4	5
30. Heart pounding	1	2	3	4	5
31. Colitis	1	2	3	4	5
32. Asthma	1	2	3	4	5
33. Indigestion	1	2	3	4	5
34. High blood pressure	1	2	3	4	5
35. Hyperventilation	1	2	3	4	5
36. Arthritis	1	2	3	4	5
37. Skin rash	1	2	3	4	5
38. Bruxism/jaw pain	1	2	3	4	5
39. Allergy	1	2	3	4	5

Source: H. Ebel et al., eds., Presidential Sports Award Fitness Manual, 197, 208, 98.

Interpretation
40–75	Low physiological symptoms of stress response	101–150	High physiological symptoms of stress response
76–100	Moderate physiological symptoms of stress response	Over 150	Excessive physiological symptoms of stress response

Personality and Stress

In identifying people who are at risk for developing cardiovascular disease, researchers believe that there is a connection between behavior pattern and risk of heart disease. People were classified as being either "Type A" or "Type B" personalities. The **Type A** person is always "on the go," never satisfied with his or her level of achievement, and appears tense, suffers from a sense of time urgency, and is competitive and impatient. In contrast, the **Type B** person is more easy-going and relaxed, more patient and satisfied with his or her level of achievement. A newer category, the **Type C** person, thrives and stays well during stress. The Type A person was believed to have a higher risk of developing cardiovascular disease. Recent research suggests that only those Type A individuals who have hostile or angry behavior patterns are at risk. Therefore, identifying the sources of anger and hostility in these people and helping them with behavior modification may allow them to cope more effectively with stress.

Type A Behavior Pattern

According to the research of Friedman and Rosenman, Type A individuals are more prone to coronary heart disease. The Type A personality possesses the following characteristics: competitive, verbally aggressive, hard-driving, unable to relax, very time conscious, easily angered, and hostile.

Read each of the statements on the following scale and check which behavior best applies to you.

This scale, based on the one developed by Friedman and Rosenman, will give you an estimate of your Type A tendencies.

Table 8-2. Assess Yourself

Directions: Answer the following questions by indicating the response that most often applies to you.

YES	NO	STATEMENT
☐	☐	1. I always feel rushed.
☐	☐	2. I find it hard to relax.
☐	☐	3. I attempt to do more and more in less and less time.
☐	☐	4. I often find myself doing more than one thing at a time.
☐	☐	5. When someone takes too long to make their point, I finish their sentence for them.
☐	☐	6. Waiting in line for anything drives me crazy.
☐	☐	7. I am always on time or early.
☐	☐	8. In a conversation, I often clench my fist and pound home important points.
☐	☐	9. I often use explosive outbursts to accentuate key points.
☐	☐	10. I am competitive at everything.
☐	☐	11. I tend to evaluate my success by translating things into numbers.
☐	☐	12. Friends tell me I have more energy than most people.
☐	☐	13. I always move, walk, and eat quickly.
☐	☐	14. I bring work home often.
☐	☐	15. I tend to get bored on vacation.
☐	☐	16. I feel guilty when I am not being "productive."
☐	☐	17. I tend to refocus other people's conversations around things that interest me.
☐	☐	18. I hurry others along in their conversations.
☐	☐	19. It is agonizing to be stuck behind someone driving too slowly.
☐	☐	20. I find it intolerable to let others do something I can do faster.

Scoring: Add up the number of items for which you checked yes. The greater the number of yes items, the more likely it is that you possess a Type A personality.

Type B Behavior

Type B behavior is the absence of Type A. While the person who exhibits Type B behavior may be ambitious and successful, he or she is generally calmer, more patient and less hurried. Of course, there are gradations within each behavior type. Most of us go back and forth between Type A and Type B as our activities and pressures vary from one day or week to the next. Type A personalities experience a higher continuous stress level than do Type Bs because they are more likely to be stress-seekers and thereby expose themselves to more challenges than do Type Bs. The response to these challenges turns on the sympathetic nervous system and increases secretions of hormones such as norepinephrine, which combine to produce elevated heart rates.

Type C Behavior and Hardiness

Research has also turned attention to those people who tend to thrive and stay well during challenge and difficulty. They are able to interpret challenge and difficulty as positive challenges or opportunities rather than as threats. They tend to be committed rather than detached or alienated. They feel in control of events and their reactions to those events withstand everyday stressors. Salvador Maddi and Suzanne Kobasa of the University of Chicago have identified "a distress resistance pattern." They call it **hardiness**, consisting of three Cs, relating to attitude or perception: challenge, commitment, and control. Type C people tend to engage in regular exercise and are involved in a number of social support groups. Robert Kriegel and Marilyn Kriegel have also identified a Type C behavior, or what they call a C zone, similar to hardiness, which consists of two of Kobasa and Maddi's three Cs, challenge and control, but replaces commitment with confidence.

The Type C person has the following pattern:

- **Challenge**. The person interprets a difficult task or change as a challenge rather than as a threat.

- **Confidence**. The person believes in his or her ability to master a difficult problem or challenge, rather than approaching it with self-doubt.

- **Commitment**. The person positively engages with his or her job, family, and friends, rather than feeling alienated.

- **Control**. The person believes in his or her ability to control events and reactions to events, rather than feeling helpless.

Stress Management

In this section, we discuss twelve useful ways to turn off stress and also a variety of relaxation techniques that are helpful in stress management. The recommendations that follow are not a universal remedy for stress but may give you some insight into dealing with stress and knowing your limits. You must know when your various frustrations, conflicts, and stresses are getting to you and take appropriate action to limit or modify them.

Turning Off Stress

Here are twelve things you can do to turn off stress:

1. Try to change how you perceive specific stress-inducing events. For example, the next time you're driving and a person in another car does something foolish, try not to perceive him or her as an enemy who is out to run you off the road but as a friend who has simply made a driving mistake.

2. Try to understand and deal with your anger. Acknowledge your anger to yourself. Learn to differentiate between levels of anger. Try to diagnose the threat that is causing you to be angry—it may be the result of a difference in values or in style and be no real threat to you at all. Finally, try letting go of anger through forgiveness and by canceling the charges against the other person.

3. Take time to relax or meditate. Utilize the relaxation techniques presented in this chapter or find a relaxing activity that you enjoy and allows you to unwind.

4. Utilize your social support system and expand your network by establishing relationships with new people or groups that may be able to give you emotional support. Share worries with someone you can trust.

5. Exercise regularly. Considerable evidence indicates that people who exercise regularly have lower arousal to stress than do people who are less fit. Exercise aids in balancing and stabilizing the physiological consequences of emotional stress, both immediately and in the long term. When you exercise, neurotransmitters in the brain, called **endorphins**, are released and produce feelings of well-being. Exercise also maintains your body systems in a fit state so that they are able to effectively handle any additional stress.

6. Eat well. Eat regular, well-balanced meals and avoid alcohol and cigarettes. Caffeine and nicotine actually produce a stress-like response by mimicking sympathetic nervous system stimulation.

7. Slow down. Learn to slow your pace of talking, walking, and eating. Take time to "smell the roses."

8. Focus on the positive and be grateful for what you do have.

9. Practice good time management by not taking on too many responsibilities or setting unrealistic deadlines. Give yourself enough time to finish tasks and learn to live with unfinished tasks.

10. Look outside of yourself by volunteering to help those less fortunate than you.

11. Laugh regularly. Laughter produces a physiological response that allows one to enter a state of relaxation and also provides a mental break from daily stressors.

12. When stress becomes too great for you to handle on your own, seek out campus resources and get help. There are counseling services available to you, support groups that you can join, and workshops to help you learn better time management skills.

Relaxation Techniques

There probably are times during the day when you just want to unwind, relax, take time out, and turn off anxiety-producing stimuli. Tension manifests itself in muscle contractions, shallow breathing, a clenched jaw, and a variety of other involuntary responses. With a little practice and patience, you can begin to free yourself of tension with a variety of relaxation techniques such as diaphragmatic breathing, meditation, progressive relaxation, autogenic training, massage, Hatha Yoga and Tai Chi. It is important to relieve the tensions in both your body and your brain so that they relax as one. Try the following relaxation techniques to see what works for you.

Diaphragmatic Breathing

Diaphragmatic breathing is a technique that combines relaxation and quieting. Opposed to a shallow breath in the upper chest, **diaphragmatic breathing** is a deep, three-part breath that gets the diaphragm muscle to move. This technique is often utilized in Lamaze classes, yoga, and Tai Chi, but can be done anywhere and anytime to produce an instant calming effect. Once mastered, diaphragmatic breathing can temporarily lower breathing from a typical

rate of 14 to 18 breaths per minute to nearly 4 breaths per minute. Try this exercise to experience it for yourself:

Assume a comfortable seated or reclining position. Place your hands on your belly and take a deep, cleansing breath through your nose. Feel your hands move as your belly expands with the breath. Exhale. Next, move your hands to your rib cage. Breathe into your belly and feel it expand completely, keep your belly expanded, and fill your ribcage. Exhale. Move your hands to rest on your upper chest. Inhale, drawing your breath deep into the belly, then feel the rib cage expand, then expand the upper chest. Exhale. Let your arms rest by your sides and continue this three-part breath. On each inhale, imagine that your entire torso is expanding with the breath. Fill the belly, then the rib cage, then the upper chest. Hold your breath in for just a moment before exhaling completely and squeezing the breath out fully at the end of the cycle. Continue until you feel more relaxed and refreshed.

Progressive Relaxation and Autogenic Training

Progressive relaxation is a technique that encourages one to learn how to recognize when he or she is bracing, or tensing, muscles. An individual will purposely contract a muscle group to learn how to recognize muscle tension and then relax it to feel the difference, progressing through the body one muscle group at a time. **Autogenic training** is a relaxation technique that encourages one to imagine the limbs and torso becoming heavy, warm, and tingling. Once muscles are able to relax, one can achieve a more relaxed state of mind. Imagery is a key element incorporated into both of these techniques and can help to establish a body-mind connection in the relaxation process. As a result, people often experience positive physiological and psychological effects, reducing the toll that stress can take on the body and the mind. The following exercise combines these relaxation techniques:

Find a quiet environment that is free of distractions. Lie on the floor in a comfortable position with a small pillow under your head and knees for support. Close your eyes and take a deep, relaxing breath. Begin by curling your toes under and tensing the muscles in your feet. Hold this for five seconds and then release for at least ten seconds. Imagine that your feet are completely relaxed, warm, and heavy. Feel them sink into the floor and relax deeper. Continue the process of tensing, relaxing, and imagining a warm and heavy sensation in each part of your body: lower legs, knees, thighs, buttocks, hips, belly, lower back, middle back, upper back, chest, shoulders, arms, hands, throat, back of the neck, face, jaw, and eyes. Imagine that your whole body feels heavy and relaxed, as if it were sinking into warm sand at the beach. Now imagine a relaxing scene, such as a beach or a lake, and place yourself in that scene. Imagine all of the details: what do you see, hear, and feel around you in this beautiful and comforting place? When you are ready, begin to bring your attention to your breath and allow it to deepen. Take a moment to notice how your body feels and if your mind is relaxed. Slowly start to take some gentle stretches to help you wake up. Continue to take several deep breaths as you return your attention to the room.

Hatha Yoga

Hatha Yoga refers to the physical practice of using bodily postures (*asanas*) and breathing techniques (*pranayama*) to create mental focus and relaxation. The goal of Yoga is to unite body, mind, and soul. Through the regular practice of Hatha Yoga, students can learn to strengthen the body while easing the mind. Hatha Yoga classes often begin and end with meditation and encourage a deep connection to the breath while practicing the asanas. **Meditation** is a relaxation technique that uses an object to focus your attention on to clear the mind, and thus relax the body. Many other relaxation techniques, such as diaphragmatic breathing, progressive relaxation, and autogenic training are often incorporated into a Hatha Yoga class. Hatha Yoga practitioners experience physiological benefits from the regulation of the nervous system, which has a calming effect on the body and on the mind. To fully experience this effect, attend a class with a certified Hatha Yoga instructor. The Sun Salutation (pictured on the following page) is an example of a flowing sequence of yoga asanas that can be used as a moving meditation. This series creates strength, flexibility, and focus as the practitioner alternates using a deep, cleansing inhale with a complete exhale as she moves fluidly from one pose to the next.

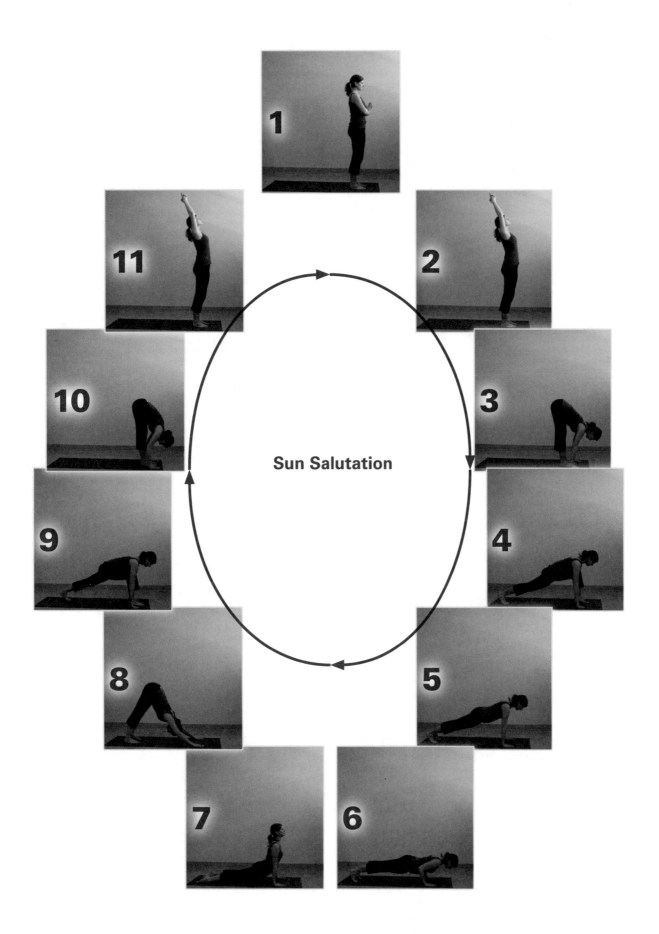

Sun Salutation

College Students and Stress

A majority of college students deal with stress on a daily basis. Pressure to perform well in school can come from parents, teachers, friends, and even oneself. Many students take on jobs to either support their lifestyle or pay for tuition. Trying to juggle school and work and find time to create meaningful and lasting relationships can place considerable stress on a college student. In addition, during the college years a young college student is faced with numerous and significant tasks such as:

a. Achieving emotional independence from family

b. Choosing and preparing for a career

c. Preparing for emotional commitment and family life

d. Developing an ethical system

Inability to juggle all these tasks can leave a college student feeling overwhelmed and almost in a state of despair. Too much stress depresses the immune system. The common health problems often seen in college health facilities, such as the flu and mono, are most likely stress-related. Second to accidents, suicide is the second leading cause of death of college students.

Student Stress Scale

The **Student Stress Scale** represents an adaptation of Holmes and Rahe's Life Event Scale. It has been modified to apply to college-age adults and should be considered a rough indication of stress levels and health consequences.

In the Student Stress Scale, each event, such as beginning or ending school, is given a score that represents the amount of readjustment a person has to make in life as a result of the change. In some studies, people with serious illness have been found to have high scores on similar scales.

To determine your stress score, add the number of points corresponding to the events you have experienced in the past twelve months. Your score indicates your life-change units (LCU). Those with 150–199 LCU have a 37% chance of developing stress-related illnesses within a year. Individuals scoring 200–299 LCU have a 79% chance of developing illness or disease.

EXPERIENCED EVENT	POINTS
1. Death of a close family member	100
2. Death of a close friend	73
3. Divorce between parents	65
4. Jail term	63
5. Major personal injury or illness	63
6. Marriage	58
7. Firing from a job	50
8. Failure of an important course	47
9. Change in health of a family member	45
10. Pregnancy	45
11. Sex problems	44
12. Serious argument with close friend	40
13. Change in financial status	39
14. Change of major	39
15. Trouble with parents	39
16. New girlfriend or boyfriend	37
17. Increase in workload at school	37
18. Outstanding personal achievement	36
19. First quarter/semester in college	36
20. Change in living conditions	31
21. Serious argument with an instructor	30
22. Lower grades than expected	29
23. Change in sleeping habits	29
24. Change in social activities	29
25. Change in eating habits	28
26. Chronic car trouble	26
27. Change in the number of family get-togethers	26
28. Too many missed classes	25
29. Change of college	24
30. Dropping of more than one class	23
31. Minor traffic violations	20
	TOTAL

Warning Signs of Stress

Selye lists stress symptoms that may represent danger signs. If you regularly experience one or more of these symptoms, you may benefit from reducing the stress in your life.

- Anxiety
- Breathlessness
- Crying
- Diarrhea and indigestion
- Dryness of throat and mouth
- Easily startled by small sounds
- Emotional tension
- Fatigue
- Feelings of weakness and dizziness
- Frequent urination
- Heart palpitations
- Impulsive behavior
- Inability to concentrate
- Increased smoking
- Insomnia
- Irritability and depression
- Loss of appetite
- Migraine headaches
- Nervous laughter
- Nervous tics
- Nightmares
- Pain in back
- Premenstrual tension or missed menstrual cycles
- Stuttering or other speech problems
- Sweating
- Trembling hands
- Vomiting

Try keeping a log of the stressors and resulting physical and psychological results you experience. Once you begin to recognize the things in your life that trigger a stress response, you can take measures toward easing that stress. For example, you can practice diaphragmatic breathing or take a yoga class at the first signs of distress. The earlier you intervene, the less likely you are to suffer from negative effects of stress. Find a stress management technique that works for you and know when to ask for help.

Summary Questions

1. How does perception play a role in stress?
2. Which personality type fairs better when encountering a stressor?
3. Think of one stressor you have encountered in the past week. Would you classify this stressor as creating eustress or distress and why?

References

Blonna, R. (2000). *Coping with Stress in a Changing World*. Second Edition. New York, NY: McGraw-Hill Publishing.

Greenberg, J.S. (2013). *Comprehensive Stress Management*. Thirteenth Edition. New York, NY: McGraw-Hill Publishing.

Greenberg, J.S. (2002). *Your Personal Stress Profile and Activity Workbook*.

Hahn, D.B. & Payne, W.A. (2005). *Focus on Health*. Seventh Edition. New York, NY: McGraw-Hill Publishing.

Iyengar, B.K.S. (1989) *The Tree of Yoga*. Boston, MA: Shambhala.

Web Sites

http://www.stress.org
American Institute of Stress

http://www.apa.org
American Psychological Association

http://www.yogaalliance.org
Yoga Alliance

http://www.yogajournal.com
Yoga Journal

Section Four

Special Topics

This section on Special Topics focuses on health-related issues not detailed in previous chapters. These topics include information on sports- and exercise-related injuries, how to select health care providers, alternative activity choices and instruction for those with disabilities, cancer, and sexually transmitted infections.

chapter 9

Special Topics
Fitness/Sports-Related Injuries
and Medical Conditions

by Louis C. Almekinders, M.D.; Sally V. Almekinders, M.Ed.

Sports participation has an inherent risk of injury. On the other hand, the health benefits of sports are significant and generally outweigh the risk of injury. Additionally, preventive measures and early injury recognition can minimize injury problems. Most injuries affect the musculoskeletal system. The musculoskeletal system includes the bones, joints, muscles, tendons, and ligaments. Tendons and ligaments are structurally very similar. Tendons serve as the connection between muscles and bones. Ligaments connect bones to bones and as such provide stability to the joints. Joints contain cartilage in order to allow the bones to move smoothly within the joint and absorb the impact of activities that load the joint. Finally, there are bursal sacs or bursae. These are thin, fluid-filled structures that help lubricate movement of skin or tendon passing over prominent bones or other tendons. Only a few injuries affect non-musculoskeletal structures such as the skin or internal organs. Sports-related injuries can be categorized into acute, chronic musculoskeletal injuries and other, more general medical problems.

Acute injuries are the result of a single event that causes damage to a part of the musculoskeletal system. Collisions, falls, and awkward movements of joints are the usual causes. Tissues can get injured when a joint is forced beyond its normal range of motion. Direct impact causes tissue to abnormally compress, creating tissue damage or contusions. Sprains, strains, fractures, and cartilage tears are common types of acute injuries each affecting different types of musculoskeletal tissues. Sprains are acute ligament injuries, whereas strains are acute muscle or tendon injuries. Fractures are injuries that are exclusively confined to the bone. Cartilage injuries occur as a result of injury to the joints. Many acute injuries require evaluation by a health-care professional. Inability to bear weight on the injured structure, obvious deformity, and immediate onset of severe swelling or bleeding are all warning signs that medical evaluation should not be delayed. Please see Table 9-1: "Comparison of Different Types of Acute Injuries" for more information. Although each type of acute injury has unique features with regards to symptoms, diagnosis, and treatment, they all have certain biologic responses

9
___
Chapter
Nine

in common. The basic contents of musculoskeletal tissues are live cells surrounded by a strong matrix. The basic ground substance of the matrix is collagen which is a long, cross-linked molecule that lends these tissues their mechanical strength. When a musculoskeletal structure is acutely injured, there is damage to the cells and surrounding matrix, along with blood vessel disruption and bleeding. The cell death, matrix injury, and bleeding is recognized by the body's defenses. The initial response of the body includes dilation of the blood vessels to bring in more blood and fluid, recruitment of inflammatory cells, and production of certain molecules, often called collectively inflammatory mediators. This initial inflammatory response creates additional swelling and pain which seems counterproductive but is in reality the initial stage of healing. The pain prevents continued use and therefore additional damage. The inflammatory cells are capable of clearing dead cells and damaged matrix. The initial inflammatory response usually peaks several days after the injury and is responsible for the worsening pain and stiffness that is often noted 2–3 days following an acute injury. Following the inflammatory phase, the body brings in new cells that repopulate the injured area, multiply, and start producing a new matrix. This phase is generally called the proliferative phase and can last several weeks. Finally, the newly produced matrix is remodeled by the surrounding cells in a new, often stronger tissue. This maturation phase can last weeks to months. As can be seen in Table 9-1, the basic approach to injuries mirrors this injury response. Initially there is rest, protection, and pain control to manage the inflammatory response. The later treatment is focused on promoting the proliferative response by rehabilitation exercises and eventually conditioning. Although many acute injuries can heal satisfactorily in this manner, the healed tissue is rarely of the same quality as the original tissue. The newly produced matrix is generally slightly different and is responsible for the scar tissue that remains in the healed area.

Chronic injuries are not the result of any single event. Chronic injuries are caused by repetitive forces that injure a structure over time. Musculoskeletal structures gradually adapt to repetitive forces by becoming stronger and better able to absorb stress placed on it. However, this adaptation process is slow. If repetitive forces are increased in intensity and/or duration too rapidly, the adaptation process is overwhelmed, the musculoskeletal tissue begins to break down, and injury ensues, not unlike the acute injuries. The breakdown can also be followed by a low-grade inflammatory response which can cause significant, often long lasting pain and disability. Tendonitis, bursitis, and stress fractures are common types of chronic injuries each affecting different types of musculoskeletal tissues. Please see Table 9-2: "Comparison of Different Types of Chronic Injuries" for more information. The general treatment approach for chronic injuries is different than acute injuries. Absolute rest and immobilization are generally not needed as the inflammatory response is often mild or even absent. Absolute rest can even be detrimental as it causes weakness, stiffness, and removes the stimulus for the proliferative and maturation responses. Relative rest is often accomplished by removing the athlete from the offending activities and continuing lower intensity exercises that stimulate healing. For instance, an injured runner should consider switching to biking or swimming while the injury heals. Although chronic injuries are often considered mild they still can take weeks to months to heal.

A common feature of all acute and chronic injuries is pain. Managing the pain should first and foremost be done by activity modifications. As pain is a natural warning mechanism, it should be used as the main guide for return to activities after injury. Pain that cannot be controlled by activity modifications can be treated by medication or local modalities. Locally, the application of ice or other cooling modalities is most commonly used. Heat is generally not advised for the treatment of injury pain. Ice should generally not be applied to bare skin. Placing a barrier such as a towel or bandage between the ice and the skin minimizes the risk of frostbite injuries to the skin. Normally, ice application lasts 15–20 minutes and can be repeated several times each day. Medication can also be helpful to control the injury pain. Several medications are available to the general public without prescription as over-the-counter (OTC) medication. Acetaminophen is a mild analgesic that is available for minor aches and pain. It is probably the OTC medication with the least amount of side-effects, although liver problems have been seen when used in high doses. Acetylsalicylic acid, ibuprofen, and naproxen are a group of OTC pain medication that belong to the group of non-steroidal anti-inflammatory drugs (NSAIDs). Besides acting as an analgesic similar to acetaminophen, they also inhibit the inflammatory response. As a result, NSAIDs can at times be more effective in controlling the pain of the inflammatory response. At the same time, NSAIDs have a larger number of possible side-effects, including stomach ulcer formation and effects on the kidney and heart.

Though some acute and chronic injuries can't be avoided as they are an inherent part of participation in sports, some may be avoided or reduced in severity. Proper warm-up and stretching prior to activity can be a key element in avoiding injury. Appropriate functional and balanced strength and conditioning programs are also important in preparing the body and its tissues for the demands of athletic endeavors.

Medical Conditions in Sports and Fitness

Besides musculoskeletal injuries as described previously, there are many medical conditions that can be precipitated by sports activities or require special considerations during sports activities. It is important to recognize some of these as they can at times result in life-threatening situations. Some of the most common conditions that fall under this heading are:

- traumatic brain injuries
- heat illness
- sudden cardiac arrest
- asthma

It is beyond the scope of this chapter to discuss these conditions in detail or address all other potential medical conditions but several of the major issues will be highlighted.

Traumatic Brain Injuries

Head injuries obviously are seen in contact sports such as American football and lacrosse, but also can occur in non-contact sports due to accidental collision and falls. It has been estimated that there are several million sports-related head injuries each year in the United States. They can range from very mild injury (frequently described as an athlete having his or her "bell rung") to concussion and even severe injury resulting in death. An initial head injury can result in severe brain injury. However, research has shown that a subsequent injury shortly after the initial injury has a very high mortality rate. This dreaded injury is frequently termed "second impact syndrome." Therefore,

it is critical that the initial injury is carefully evaluated and athletes are kept out of play until it is clear that the initial injury has resolved. Signs of significant injury requiring in-depth evaluation and prolonged absence from the sport are: any temporary loss of consciousness, retrograde amnesia (not remembering the circumstances prior to the injury), confusion and lack of balance or motor skills. In general, evaluation of any suspected head injury should be done by professionals trained in the sideline evaluation of these injuries. Return to play decisions can be very difficult, even for an experienced professional. Often it is recommended to not return to play the same day and perform serial evaluations over time as the effect of the impact may not be immediately evident. In addition, more sophisticated neuropsychological testing can be done in a clinical setting that is not possible at the sidelines. Avoiding the second impact syndrome is important for short-term injury management. However, it also appears more and more evident that repeated minor traumatic brain injuries over a long period of time can have a detrimental effect on brain function later in life. This has particularly become a concern for professional athletes in contact sports who have been shown to develop degenerative brain disorders, such as dementia. As a result, prevention has become an important part of this issue through rule changes, helmet design, and limiting the total number of injuries for an athlete over a lifetime.

Heat Illness

Exercise and sports require energy production in the muscle, and heat is a normal by-product of the metabolic process. The heat is dissipated through convection, radiation into the environment and particularly the cooling effect of sweat evaporation. If the ambient temperature and/or the humidity are high, these processes become impaired and heat illness can become a serious risk. There are seemingly several degrees of heat illness as described in Table 9-3. Heat stroke can be fatal. Warning signs include confusion and a paradoxical decrease in sweating. If there is any suspicion that these type of symptoms are developing, cooling by any means possible should be initiated.

Sudden Cardiac Arrest

Sudden cardiac arrest is the leading cause of death in young athletes. It is usually characterized by a sudden collapse of an athlete who previously seemed to be doing well. In young athletes it is usually caused by a pre-existing heart abnormality called hypertrophic cardiomyopathy. The heart is enlarged and thickened, which eventually can cause a restriction of flow through the heart. Cardiac arrest can also be caused by a direct blow to the chest if the blow occurs at a very specific portion of the heart cycle. This is called commotion cordis. Finally, older athletes are at risk from cardiac arrest due to myocardial infarction as coronary arteries may be affected by atherosclerosis. Any athlete that collapses on the playing field or court should be checked for breathing and pulse. If absent, cardiopulmonary resuscitation should be initiated while Emergency Medical Services (EMS) is contacted. An automated external defibrillator (AED) should be looked for and used as soon as possible since survival is directly correlated with the rapid use of these devices. Identification of athletes with heart abnormalities in a pre-participation physical examination is recommended but is not always easy. Any athlete with a personal family history of collapse or chest pain should have a more in-depth cardiac evaluation prior to sports participation.

Asthma

Asthma is an airway disease where airflow can become restricted, creating shortness of breath, wheezing and coughing. It is thought to affect as much as 22 million people in this country. Asthma tends to be symptomatic as "asthma attacks." These attacks can be triggered by a variety of events including allergens, cold air and exercise. Obviously, an athlete affected by exercise-induced asthma can have severe problems with sport participation. Although some attacks may be obvious, others may be more subtle and not recognized as such. Athletes can be frustrated by declining performance due to unrecognized asthma. Prevention is key in exercise-induced asthma. A structured warm-up prior to competition is very important, especially in a cold environment. Medication can often be used to prevent attacks while, if needed, different medication can also treat ongoing attacks. Careful adherence to a medication regimen is generally successful in preventing attacks.

Table 9-1. Comparison of Different Types of Acute Injuries

INJURY TYPE	TISSUE INVOLVED	DEGREE	SIGNS	TREATMENT
Sprain	Ligament/Joints	**1st Degree** • Minimal pain/swelling • No structural damage • No joint instability **2nd Degree** • Moderate pain/swelling • Some structural damage • Some joint instability • Difficulty bearing weight **3rd Degree** • Severe pain/swelling • Complete ligament rupture • Pop/snap felt • Joint instability • Difficulty bearing weight strain	• Immediate onset of pain • Often rapid onset of swelling • Tender upon palpation • Discoloration • Decreased range of motion at the involved joint • Difficulty bearing weight or performing everyday activity with involved joint • Feelings of instability	• Rest, ice, compression, elevation (RICE) • Protective bracing to protect involved joint • Possible surgery • Range of motion exercises • Strengthening of muscles surrounding involved joint to improve active stabilization
Strain	Muscle/Tendon	**1st Degree** • Muscle is tender/painful when used • No structural damage **2nd Degree** • Moderate pain/swelling • Some structural damage • Difficult to use involved muscle • Discoloration **3rd Degree** • Severe pain/swelling • Complete muscle rupture • Use of involved muscle is impossible	• Immediate onset of pain and difficulty using involved muscle • May feel a snap/pop • Muscle spasm • Discoloration • Tender upon palpation • Partial or complete loss of function	• Rest, ice, compression, elevation (RICE) • Anti-inflammatory medications • Analgesics • Range of motion exercises and stretching as pain subsides • Strengthening of involved muscle once full range of motion is restored
Fracture	Bone	**Simple and Non-Displaced** • Simple crack in the bone • No displacement **Simple and Displaced** • Simple crack in the bone • Displacement of bones from their normal position **Comminuted** • Several cracks in the bone • Multiple bone fragments • Usually displaced **Compound or Open** • Bone fragment pierces the skin • Severe pain/tenderness • Deformity of displaced fractures • Bleeding of compound fractures	• May feel pop/snap • Severe pain/tenderness • Deformity in displaced fracture • Bleeding in compound fracture	• Immediate immobilization • Transportation to a facility capable of taking x-rays of the injured area • Cast or brace for non-displaced fractures • Reduction of displaced fracture • Surgery of all compound fractures to avoid infection and to reduce displaced fragments

Table 9-2. Comparison of Different Types of Chronic Injuries

INJURY TYPE	TISSUE INVOLVED	SIGNS AND SYMPTOMS	TREATMENT	COMMON EXAMPLES
Tendonitis	Tendon	• Pain with use in and around the tendon • Tenderness with palpation of the tendon • Occasional swelling or thickening of the tendon	• Rest: Decrease the intensity/duration of the exercise until pain subsides. Complete rest may not be ideal as it takes away the stimulus of the tendon to adapt and heal. Often finding alternative exercises that still use the injured structure is ideal. • Anti-inflammatory medication • Ice • Stretching • Occasionally, a physician may use corticosteroid injections. Must be used with caution as these tend to weaken tendon and increase the likelihood of complete tendon rupture, especially in weight-bearing tendons (Achilles tendon among others).	• Achilles tendonitis • Rotator cuff tendonitis • Tennis elbow • Patella tendonitis or jumper's knee
Stress Fracture	Bone	• Gradually increasing pain over a bone, eventually leading to severe pain that forces athlete to stop exercising • Palpable tenderness on the bone at the site of the stress fracture • Most common in distance runners	• Rest: Avoidance of the aggravating impact activity. Cross training with a non-weight bearing exercise is good to maintain fitness level. • Total non-weight bearing or immobilization is rarely needed. • Sometimes surgery is needed to stabilize poor healing stress fractures.	• Forefoot stress fracture • Tibia or shin bone stress fracture • Hip stress fractures
Bursitis	Bursa	• Swelling or thickening of bursa • Palpable tenderness around the bursa	• Rest: Avoidance of the aggravating activity. Cross training is good to maintain fitness level. • Stretch the involved tendon causing the friction over the bursa. • Anti-inflammatory medication • Protective padding to shield bursa from further irritation	• Achilles bursitis • Shoulder bursitis

Table 9-3. Forms of Exertional Heat Illness

CONDITION	PREVENTION	SIGNS AND SYMPTOMS	TREATMENT
Heat Illness	• Gradual acclimatization • Wear proper, light clothing • Proper hydration • Maintain proper body weight • Be aware of temperature/humidity and adjust workouts accordingly	**Heat Cramps**	
		• Sudden painful contraction of muscle tissue • Dehydration • Mineral imbalance	• Stretching of involved muscle tissue • Fluid and electrolyte replenishment • Rest
		Heat Exhaustion	
		• Feeling of weakness • Fatigue • Occasional collapse without loss of consciousness • Profuse sweating	• Fluid and electrolyte replenishment • Cooling the body off • Rest
		Heat Stroke	
		• Serious emergency • Collapse • Confusion • Loss of consciousness possible • Elevated core temperature • Decreased or no sweating • Complete shutdown of body's defensive mechanism against overheating	• Immediate cooling through removal of clothes, shade, ice or fanning • Call 911 for immediate professional emergency care

Summary Questions

1. What is the basic difference between an acute and a chronic athletic injury in terms of their causes?

2. Describe the general, biologic responses of the body to an acute musculoskeletal injury.

3. Define the degrees of injury that are possible in an acute strain or sprain.

4. Describe the general treatment approach of a chronic, overuse musculoskeletal injury.

5. Why is it important that a head injury is fully resolved before allowing an athlete to return to play?

References

Casa, D.J.; Guskiewicz, K.M.; Anderson, S.A.; et al. (2012) *National Athletic Trainers' Association Position Statement: Preventing Sudden Death in Sports*. J Athl Train 47: 96–118

Miller, M.D.; Thompson, S.R. (2014) *DeLee & Drez's Orthapaedic Sports Medicine*, 4th Edition

O'Connor, F.G.; Casa, D.J.; Davis, B.A. (2013) *ACSM's Sports Medicine. A Comprehensive Review*. Wolters Kluwwer/Lippincott, Williams & Wilkins

Pescatello, L.S.; Arena, R.; Riebe, D.; Thompson, P.D. (eds). (2013) *ACSM's Guidelines for Exercise testing and Prescription*. 9th Edition. Wolters Kluwer/Lippincott, Williams & Wilkins

Prentice, W.E. (2012) *Essentials of Athletic Injury Management*. McGraw-Hill Higher Education.

Starkey, C.; Brown, S.D.; Ryan, J. (2015) *Orthopedic & Athletic Injury Examination Handbook*. 3rd edition. F.A. Davis Co.

Web Sites

http://nccam.nih.gov/
National Center for Complimentary and Alternative Medicine (NCCAM)

http://nccih.nih.gov
National Institutes of Health/National Library of Medicine

http://orthoinfo.aaos.org
American Academy of Orthopaedic Surgeons

http://www.sportsmed.org/AOSSMIMIS/Members/Patient/
American Orthopaedic Society for Sports Medicine

http://www.acsm.org/access-public-information
American College of Sports Medicine

chapter 10

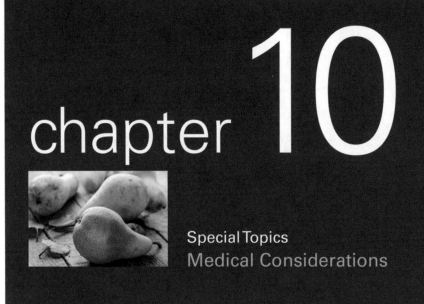

Special Topics
Medical Considerations

10
Chapter
Ten

by Ed Remen, MS; Kari Lewis, Ed.D.

Who's Your Doctor?

Each of us shoulders the responsibility of our own health care and quality of life. This can be a very complex and confusing task. It can be made easier for us if we know where to turn for information, services, and support. Having access to professional health care practitioners is an important element in health maintenance. Selecting the right health care professional is an important decision that will benefit you for the rest of your life.

Today we have a lot of options for our medical care. We must have the knowledge to be proactive in making careful and educated decisions when it comes to our health care.

Conventional Western Medicine is based on scientifically proven methods, tests, and trials. It is practiced by holders of Doctor of Medicine (M.D.) or Doctor of Osteopathic Medicine (D.O.) degrees and by their allied health professionals, who can provide certain limited aspects of direct patient care. These include family nurse practitioners (FNP) and physician assistants (PA).

As it relates to fitness advice, several different providers can provide advice, assistance, and care. Primary care providers or family physicians are often available for the initial advice on how to initiate and continue a medically safe fitness program. Based on their advice, licensed personal trainers can devise a specific fitness program. For patients with more complicated medical conditions such as heart disease or diabetes, a specialist such as a cardiologist or internist may have to get involved for their exercise prescription.

When fitness-related injuries occur, the primary care physician or family physician can also be a choice for an initial consultation. Acute on-field evaluation and management is generally done by an athletic trainer. For complex or more severe musculoskeletal injuries, an orthopaedic surgeon will generally have to become involved with the care and treatment. During the recovery and rehabilitation, a physical therapist or athletic trainer can supervise a recovery program. All of the above-mentioned providers have training and licenses that are controlled by federal and/or state agencies. This assures a certain level of proficiency and expertise. In addition, prescription medications and many other therapies used by these providers have gone through rigorous scientific testing before they were released by federal agencies, such as the Food and Drug Administration (FDA).

Health care practices and products that are not presently considered to be part of conventional medicine are called **complementary and alternative medicine** (CAM). As we grow more frustrated with the limitations of conventional medicine, millions of Americans are turning to CAM for their healing. CAM includes a wide range of healing philosophies, techniques, and therapies. The practices of yoga, spirituality, relaxation, massage, acupuncture, homeopathy, chiropractic, herbalism, naturopathy, and magnetic therapy are just a few. Each offers a different approach to treatment. However, we often don't know which approaches to trust, or what accounts for their effectiveness, and many of our conventional medicine doctors are not able to tell us. The National Center for Complementary and Alternative Medicine (NCCAM) was established to examine new methods of healing.

A new model of medicine has emerged. It is a "healing partnership" that encourages teamwork to make patients well and a personalized plan to keep them that way. This is called "**Integrated Medicine**," a collaborative, cross-disciplinary approach to patient care. It is the integration of all the available resources to meet the full health care needs of the patient. Each of us is always changing and unique. We are a whole person, biological, psychological, and spiritual, in a total social and ecological environment, and we will require different approaches to our health care needs.

Integrative medicine combines medical evaluations and consultation, workshops, health planning, and coaching with many therapeutic services. Ideally, we will have informed doctors working with proactive patients who are both aware of the patient's individual needs and can draw from the many healing resources to establish an effective plan for lifelong health.

The following resource guide will help you with this selection. Ultimately you are responsible for your own well-being. Your health should last a lifetime.

Types of Health Care Providers

Acupuncturists: Follow a health care practice that originated in traditional Chinese medicine. It involves inserting needles at specific points on the body, in the belief that this will help improve the flow of the body's energy and thereby help the body achieve and maintain health.

Anesthesiologist: A doctor who is primarily concerned with administering the various drugs that keep patients from feeling pain during surgery.

Cardiologist: A doctor that diagnoses and treats patients suffering from diseases of the heart, lungs, and blood vessels. They educate patients on preventing heart problems and living a heart-healthy lifestyle.

Chiropractor (*DC*): Believes that many diseases and ailments are related to misalignments of the vertebrae and emphasize the manipulation of the spinal column. Chiropractors use a type of hands-on therapy called manipulation (adjustment) as their core clinical procedure.

Dentist: A practitioner who specializes in diseases of the teeth, gums, and oral cavity.

Oral/Maxillofacial Surgeon: A dentist that focuses on the diagnosis and surgical treatment of diseases, injuries, and deformities of the teeth, mouth, and jaw. An oral surgeon removes wisdom teeth, repairs broken jaws, and treats a range of other conditions.

Orthodontist: A dentist who specializes in the correction and prevention of teeth irregularities.

Dermatologist: A doctor that treats disorders and diseases of the skin, ranging from warts to acne to skin cancers.

Endocrinologist: A doctor that is concerned with hormonal and metabolic disorders. They treat problems with the thyroid, pituitary and adrenal glands, as well as nutritional disorders, sexual disorders, and problems such as diabetes and hypertension.

Gastroenterologist: A doctor that treats conditions of the digestive system. They diagnose and treat disorders of the stomach, intestines, bowels, and other structures, such as the liver, gall bladder, pancreas, and esophagus.

General Surgeon: Doctors that practice all types of common surgeries involving any part of the body.

Gynecologist/Obstetrician (*OBGYNs*): Is the field of medicine devoted to conditions specific to women. Obstetrics is the care of a woman during pregnancy and during and after childbirth. Gynecology is the study and care of the female reproductive system.

Hematologist: The medical specialist concerned with blood and the blood system. They treat blood diseases such as cancer, lymphoma, serious anemia, and sickle cell disease.

Homeopaths: Practice an alternative medical system that was invented in Germany. Small, highly diluted quantities of medicinal substances are given to cure symptoms, when the same substances given at higher or more concentrated doses would actually cause those symptoms.

Immunologist: Doctors that are concerned with disorders of the immune system and allergies as well as the body's reaction to foreign substances. They treat hay fever, asthma, hives, and other abnormal responses to allergens that range from dust and food to animals and chemicals.

Infectious disease: A doctor specializing in infectious diseases diagnoses and treats patients affected by illnesses ranging from pneumonia to salmonella to AIDS.

Licensed Clinical Social Worker (*LCSWs*): Are trained and state-licensed to provide various types of counseling and support.

Magnetic Therapist: Relies on magnetic energy to promote healing. This is an unconventional treatment.

Massage Therapist: Uses the techniques of rubbing or kneading body parts to treat ailments. Muscles and connective tissue are manipulated to enhance function of those tissues and promote relaxation and well-being.

Naturopaths: Follow an alternative medical system in which they work with natural healing forces within the body, with a goal of helping the body heal from disease and attain better health. Practices may include dietary modifications, massage, exercise, acupuncture, and various other interventions.

Neonatologist: A doctor devoted to the care and treatment of infants up to six weeks old. They treat all medical problems that can affect newborn babies.

Nephrologists: A doctor that treats kidney disorders, diabetes, renal failure, and other illnesses. Treatments can range from dialysis to kidney transplants.

Neurologist: Doctors that treat diseases of the nervous system. A neurologist assists patients who have stroke complications, head injuries, epilepsy, Alzheimer's disease, and other afflictions of the brain and spinal cord.

Nurse: A health care practitioner who assists in the diagnosis and treatment of health problems and provides many services to patients in a variety of settings.

Nurse Specialties

Certified Nurse Midwives (CNMs): Are RNs who have completed an advanced course of study and are certified by the American College of Nurse-Midwives. A midwife is trained to care for women during pregnancy, labor, and the postnatal period, conduct normal deliveries, and to care for newborn babies under normal conditions.

Certified Registered Nurse Anesthetist (CRNAs): Are RNs with graduate training in the field of anesthesia.

Clinical Nurse Specialist (CNSs): Are RNs who have graduate training in a specialized clinical field, such as cardiac, psychiatric, or community health.

Licensed Practical Nurse (LPNs): Are state-licensed caregivers who have been trained to care for the sick.

Nurse Practitioners (NPs): Are RNs who have completed additional courses and specialized training in primary care. The profession includes family (FNP), pediatric (PNP), adult (ANP), and geriatric (GNP) specialties. In some states NPs can prescribe medications.

Registered Nurse (RNs): Has graduated from a nursing program and has passed state board examinations, and are licensed by the state.

Oncologist: Doctor that specializes in using various medications to treat and manage patients with cancer and some other diseases that resist treatment.

Ophthalmologist: A doctor devoted to the care of the eye and the treatment of diseases that affect eyes and vision. They diagnose and treat abnormalities of the eye and perform surgery on the eye.

Opticians: Are not medical doctors. They make or sell corrective eyewear.

Optometrists: Are not medical doctors. They test vision and prescribe corrective lenses.

Orthopedic Surgeon: A doctor concerned with the prevention and correction of muscular or skeletal injuries and abnormalities. They treat complex conditions and injuries as well as broken bones, severe muscle sprains, and knee and other joint injuries. They also perform joint replacements.

Osteopath (*DO*): Doctors of osteopathic medicine. Are medical practitioners specializing in musculoskeletal problems. They are trained in conventional medicine and additional training in manipulative measures.

Otolaryngologist (*ENT*): A doctor that focuses on the ears, nose, and throat. They diagnose and treat disorders from the shoulders up, with the exception of the eyes and brain. They may deal with hearing loss, tonsillitis, and nasal obstructions.

Pediatrician: Doctors that care for infants, children, and teenagers. They are often the first doctors children see.

Physician Assistant (*PA*): Is trained in the family practice model for a primary care role. They treat most standard cases of care.

Podiatrist (*DPM*): Attend colleges of podiatric medicine, and treat problems of the foot. They diagnose and treat maladies of the foot and ankle by medical, surgical, or mechanical means. Podiatrists with advanced training also do various types of foot surgery.

Primary Care Physician (*MD*): A doctor who usually specializes in family practice or internal medicine. They are generalist, and typically the patient's first contact for health care.

Psychiatrist: A doctor that diagnoses and treats mental, emotional, and behavioral disorders. They prescribe appropriate medication and do therapy to treat a variety of conditions from depression to schizophrenia.

Psychologist: Are health care professionals with an advanced academic degree called a Ph.D. They deal with mental processes, both normal and abnormal, and their effects upon human behavior. This involves the diagnosis, treatment, and prevention of mental and emotional disorders.

Pulmonologist: A doctor that treats diseases of the respiratory system. These physicians treat pneumonia, bronchitis, emphysema, asthma, cancer, and other disorders of the lungs and respiratory system.

Radiologist: A doctor that uses radioactive equipment, including X-ray machines and related procedures (ultrasound, MRI, CT), to diagnose and treat diseases and injuries.

Rheumatologist: A doctor that treats a range of conditions, from athletic injuries to arthritis, lupus, and rheumatic fever.

Urologist: A doctor that treats disorders of the male and female urinary tracts and the male genital tract.

Adapted Physical Education

Adapted Physical Education offers education, information, and training for those individuals that require modifications for physical activity. An individual's health condition may require physical education in an Adapted Physical Education class or he/she may participate in the regular physical education classes with minor modifications.

Health Conditions That Might Warrant Adapted Physical Education

1. Anemia
2. Arthritis
3. Asthma
4. Cardiovascular problems
5. Cystic fibrosis
6. Diabetes
7. Epilepsy
8. Kidney disorders
9. Muscular disorders
10. Obesity
11. Paralysis

Medication Considerations

Please inform your physical education instructor if you are taking medication for which side effects may be exacerbated due to physical activity.

- Diuretics—Diuretics may be used to manage obesity, heart disease, high blood pressure, and other conditions. When engaged in vigorous exercise or exercise in hot, humid conditions, the exerciser should consume water frequently. Diuretics may cause hypovolemia (excessive fluid loss) and hypokalemia (diminished blood volume, causing serious depletion of potassium). Both of these are life threatening.
  Watch for these signs: dizziness, weakness, and muscle cramps.

- Seizure Drugs—These drugs may cause poor reaction time, lack of coordination, and attention problems.

- Asthma—Drugs for asthma typically dilate the bronchial tubes and may create an increase in heart rate. Be sure to monitor your heart rate frequently if you use drugs to treat asthma.

- Blood pressure—Drugs that are used to decrease blood pressure may also mask the intensity of physical activity. Therefore, the usual methods of monitoring heart rate (i.e., counting the pulse or using a heart rate monitor) may be an inaccurate measure of the intensity of the workout. If you take alpha- and/or beta-blocker drugs, use the rating of perceived exertion (RPE) scale or "talk test" to monitor your heart rate.

- Drugs for Attention Deficit Hyperactivity Disorder (ADHD) may have the following adverse side effects, which could affect physical fitness training: anorexia, nausea, dizziness, pulse changes (up or down), tachycardia, and cardiac arrhythmia.

Exercise Guidelines

Anemia

- Individuals with mild to moderate anemia do not need restrictions for physical activity.

- Anaerobic activities are best for individuals with anemia.

- Aerobic activities tend to cause undue fatigue because of the lowered blood oxygen levels.

- Severe anemia may cause enlargement of the liver or spleen and contraindicates all but very mild exercise.

Arthritis

- Rheumatoid arthritis is generally most problematic early in the day and osteoarthritis typically becomes more painful later in the day. Select physical activity during the time of day that you are most pain-free.

- Movement and activity is essential because sitting for long periods of times puts stress on the joints.

- Three types of physical training are recommended: range of motion, aerobic exercise, and strength training.

- Prior to exercise use heat or ice as needed and/or recommended by your physician.

- Warm up gradually with low-intensity exercise.

- Swimming is an excellent non-weight bearing activity that can also increase flexibility; other non-weight bearing activities such as bicycling and rowing are also recommended.

- Weight lifting is recommended in order to increase lean tissue and maintain stability in the joints.

Asthma

- A gradual aerobic warm-up helps the airways adjust slowly to the increased demand placed on them.

- Anaerobic activity (short bursts of energy/speed) workouts may be preferable to an aerobic workout.

- Exercising in a warm, humid environment is recommended (swimming is an excellent choice) unless you experience adverse reactions to mold or chlorine.

- If exercising outdoors, avoid those time periods when pollen counts are high.

- Monitor your exercise intensity with the "talk test."

Cardiovascular Problems

- The individual with a cardiovascular problem is encouraged to consider the "ABCDEF plan," taking into account severity and/or frequency of symptoms, when exercising:

  - Angina

  - Breathing difficulty

  - Color change, bluish or pale

  - Dizziness

  - Edema, fluid retention and swelling of extremities

  - Fatigue

Cystic Fibrosis

- Scuba diving is contraindicated.

- If cystic fibrosis is severe, the individual may be at risk for an increased loss of fluid during exercise.

- A heart rate monitor is recommended so that the individual exercises within a specified heart rate range.

Diabetes

- Be sure to have a detailed medical exam before beginning any exercise program.

- Individuals with Type 1 diabetes should avoid exercise if their fasting glucose levels are more than 250 mg/dl and ketosis is present or if their glucose levels are over 300 mg/dl.

- Monitor blood glucose before and after exercise and eat enough carbohydrates to avoid hypoglycemia.

- Follow the ACSM guidelines for frequency, intensity, and duration of aerobic exercise in order to maintain body weight and body composition.

Epilepsy

- There is no evidence that intense physical activity increases the likelihood of a seizure.

- If you have been experiencing seizures, be sure to exercise with a partner, and if you are weight lifting, avoid doing free weight lifts in which the motion takes the weight over your head or chest.

- Always swim with a partner.

- Gymnastics requires a spotter when on the high bar, balance beam, parallel bars, and trampoline.

- Boxing is contraindicated and "heading" the ball in soccer is discouraged.

Kidney Disorders

- For first-time exercisers, begin with a graduated exercise program. Exercise aerobically for 10 minutes (if you are an individual on dialysis, be sure to exercise on non-dialysis days), and then increase the length of exercise by one to three minutes per week.

- Participate in weight training—keep a journal to monitor your progress and keep track of becoming fatigued.

- If you are on dialysis, be sure to monitor your fluid intake (liquids and in foods you eat) and adjust your workout accordingly (i.e., level of intensity, and whether you work out inside or outside) if excess fluid is building up in your body.

Muscular Disorders

- The goal for the individual with a muscular disorder is to maintain function for as long as possible. Therefore, avoid activities that create fatigue or pain.

- Allow yourself to have frequent rest breaks during activity. Interval training is preferred to continuous aerobic activity.

- Be flexible with your workout schedule so that you can work out when you feel most rested.

Obesity

- The individual that is obese should select non-weight bearing activities for aerobic activities; the activity should be strenuous enough to elevate the heart rate to the target heart rate range.

- The individual should participate in weight training to build lean tissue, which in turn will increase his/her metabolism.

- Be sure to acclimate to hot, humid weather and drink plenty of water before, during, and after activity.

- Wear light, loose-fitting clothing.

Orthostatic Hypotension

- The individual should avoid exercises/workouts that require frequent body position changes, i.e., from lying to a sitting or standing position.

- The individual should attempt to keep his/her head in the same position when exercising.

- When the individual has completed an exercise session, he/she should allow about five minutes to cool down and to allow the heart rate to return to a more normal state.

Paralysis

- A number of assistive devices are available so that the person with paralysis can participate as fully as possible in physical fitness classes.

- When the lower body is affected, the individual can utilize upper body weights and an arm ergometer. The exercising heart rate will generally be 10–20 beats per minute less than for an exercise

that works the large muscles of the body; therefore, monitor the heart rate using the rating of perceived exertion (RPE).

- Exercising in water is excellent for individuals with paralysis or limited use of limbs.

Summary Questions

1. How does CAM affect your healing chances?

2. What is Integrated Medicine?

3. What is Conventional Western Medicine and who may practice it?

4. As a proactive patient, what would be your plan for lifelong health?

References

Sherrill, C. (2003). *Adapted Physical Activity, Recreation, and Sport* (6th ed.). Boston, MA: McGrawHill. Auxter, I.D.; Pyfer, J.; & Huettig, C. (1997). *Principles and Methods of Adapted Physical Education and Recreation* (8th ed.). St. Louis, MO: Mosby-Year Book.

Web Sites

http://nccam.nih.gov/
National Center for Complementary and Alternative Medicine (NCCAM)

http://www.acsm.org
American College of Sports Medicine

http://www.ama-assn.org
American Medical Association

http://www.almaholistic.com/
American Holistic Medical Association (NHMA)

http://www.eatright.org
American Dietetic Association

chapter 11

Special Topics
Cabber

by Joy Kagendo, M.Ed.

Cancer is the second leading cause of death in the United States next to cardiovascular diseases. According to the National Center for Health Statistics, 14.5 million Americans were living with cancer as of 2014. A total of 1,685,210 cancer cases and 596,690 deaths are projected to occur in the U.S. in 2016. Cigarette smoking alone accounts for 188,800 yearly cancer deaths.

The American Cancer Society estimates 61,000 cases of carcinoma in situ of the female breast cancer and 68,480 cases of melanoma in situ (noninvasive) will be diagnosis in 2016. Upon diagnosis, nearly 65% of these individuals will live five years after diagnosis. This 5-year period, known as relative survivability, includes individuals living 5 years, cancer-free, in remission or under treatment. Mortality rates from cancer are higher in men than women. African Americans have the highest rate of cancer deaths and Asian Americans have the lowest reported rate of cancer deaths.

11
Chapter Eleven

Cancer Statistics 2016

Estimated New Cases

MALES

Prostate	180,890	21%
Lung & bronchus	117,920	14%
Colon & Rectum	70,820	8%
Urinary bladder	58,950	7%
Melanoma of the skin	46,870	6%
Non-Hodgkin lymphoma	40,170	5%
Kidney & renal pelvis	39,650	5%
Oral cavity & pharynx	34,780	4%
Leukemia	34,090	4%
Liver & intrahepatic bile duct	28,410	3%
All Sites	**841,390**	**100%**

FEMALES

Breast	246,660	29%
Lung & bronchus	106,470	13%
Colon & Rectum	63,670	8%
Uterine corpus	60,050	7%
Thyroid	49,350	6%
Non-Hodgkin lymphoma	32,410	4%
Melanoma of the skin	29,510	3%
Leukemia	26,050	3%
Pancreas	25,400	3%
Kidney & renal pevis	23,050	3%
All Sites	**843,820**	**100%**

Estimated Deaths

MALES

Lung & bronchus	85,920	27%
Prostate	26,120	8%
Colon & Rectum	26,020	8%
Pancreas	21,450	7%
Liver & intrahepatic bile duct	18,280	6%
Leukemia	14,130	4%
Esophagus	12,720	4%
Urinary bladder	11,820	4%
Non-Hodgkin lymphoma	11,520	4%
Brain & other nervous system	9,440	3%
All Sites	**314,290**	**100%**

FEMALES

Lung & bronchus	72,160	26%
Breast	40,450	14%
Colon & Rectum	23,170	8%
Pancreas	20,330	7%
Ovary	14,240	5%
Uterine corpus	10,470	4%
Leukemia	10,270	4%
Liver & intrahepatic bile duct	8,890	3%
Non-Hodgkin lymphoma	8,630	3%
Brain & other nervous system	6,610	2%
All Sites	**281,400**	**100%**

©Hayden-McNeil, LLC

Source: American Cancer Society.

Causes of Cancer

The process to eradicate cancer has been slow. There is no single explanation for this phenomenon but contributing factors include: aging population, tobacco use, high-fat diet, pollution, lack of health insurance for the poor and underserved, and delays in early diagnosis. Most researchers are optimistic that new pharmacological agents and vaccines to prevent and treat cancer will be discovered. The term "cancer" is derived from the Latin word "crab" because it seemed to creep in all directions throughout the body. Cancer is not a single disease but rather a large group of more than 100 different diseases characterized by uncontrolled growth and spread of abnormal cells. The causes of cancer are numerous and complex. The development of cancer, for each person, probably derives from many risk factors and cellular proliferation occurring over time.

Cancer occurs when a gene cell fails to do its job. The body depends on various cells to perform specific prescribed functions. When the cells fail to perform as prescribed, the body begins to deteriorate and the cells are no longer protected by the immune system. Cancer is therefore a disease caused by cell irregularity. When gene cells that control specialization, replication, DNA repair, and tumor suppression fail to do their job, they become cancer-causing genes, or oncogenesis. Three possible causes of this gene alteration are genetic mutations, viral infections, and carcinogens. Carcinogens are cancer-causing agents such as tobacco, chemicals, toxic waste, and polluted air and water.

Cancer Staging

Oncologists stage cancer based on the extent of the spread from point of origin to distance locations, a process known as metastasis. Staging is important as it helps oncologists plan appropriate treatment and understand the extent of the disease or cause. Perhaps the most common staging system is the TNM system. T stands for the extent of the tumor, N stands for the extent of the tumor to the lymph nodes, and M stands for the existence of metastasis. A number is then added to each letter to indicate the extent of the tumor and or size.

a.   Stage 0—this is referred to as carcinoma in situ, which means the cancer is localized and remains in its point of origin.

b.   Stage I, II, and III—indicate the severity of the disease, larger tumor sizes, and spread to the lymph nodes.

c.   Stage IV—indicates the spread of cancer to another organ.

Cancer Cells

Cancer cells (malignant tumors) differ from non-cancerous cells (benign tumors) in four ways:

1.   Cancer cells have an infinite life expectancy compared to non-cancerous cells. They have the capability to produce the enzyme telomerase which blocks normal cell life expectancy.

2.   Cancer cells lack the contact inhibition mechanism; several cells can occupy one location at the same time.

3.   Cancer cells do not have cellular cohesiveness and as such cannot stick to their home-base. They have the ability to spread to distant locations through metastasis.

4.   Cancer cells have the ability to demand extra blood supply from the circulatory system thus

allowing them to metastasize through the routes. This is known as angiogenesis.

Types of Cancer

Cancers are classified according to their point of origin in the body.

Carcinoma—originates from the skin, nose, mouth, throat, stomach, breasts, lungs, kidneys, and other soft tissues. About 85% of all malignant tumors are carcinomas.

Sarcoma—originates from connective tissue such as bones, ligaments, cartilage, and tendons. Only 2% of malignant tumors are sarcomas.

Leukemia—originates from blood and blood-forming cells. Leukemia is evident in immature white blood cell formation.

Melanoma—originates from melanin-containing cells of the skin. Melanoma is more pronounced in individuals with prolonged sun-exposure. There have been recent increases in this form of cancer which can be very aggressive and deadly.

Lymphoma—originates from lymphatic tissues and other immune system tissues. They include lymphosarcoma and Hodgkin's disease. They are characterized by abnormal white cell formation.

Hepatoma—originates from cells of the liver. Hepatoma is often seen in individuals with sclerotic livers, although not directly linked to alcohol use.

Lung Cancer

Lung cancer is the leading cause of cancer deaths in both men and women and only 15 percent of individuals diagnosed with the disease survive five years after diagnosis. This is due to the fact that by the time symptoms appear and diagnosis is made, it is often too late. In 2016, 224,390 lung cancer cases will be diagnosed, and 158,080 deaths will occur. Lung cancer accounts for 38% of all cancer deaths. Symptoms include a persistent cough, blood-streaked sputum, shortness of breath or wheezing, chest pain, unusual weight loss, and fatigue.

Risk factors include:

- Genetic predisposition

- Cigarette smoking (single most preventable risk factor)

Cigarette smoking is the single most preventable risk factor for lung cancer. According to the National Cancer Institute, 87 percent of all reported lung cancer cases are from smokers. Among nonsmokers, radon is the most common agent known to cause lung cancer.

Breast Cancer

Breast cancer is second to lung cancer as the leading cause of cancer deaths among women. It is the most common cancer site in women. According to the National Cancer Institute, one in eight women will develop breast cancer in their lifetime. In 2016, about 246,600 women and 2,600 men will be diagnosed with invasive breast cancer. An estimated 40,890 breast cancer deaths (40,450 women, 440 men) are expected in 2016. Deaths from breast cancer declined among white women by 1.9% and among Black women by 1.4%. This decline is due to early detection and awareness.

Prevention includes (1) early detection through breast self-exams, clinical exams, and mammography, (2) lifestyle changes, (3) knowing one's family history, and (4) prophylactic mastectomy. Prophylactic mastectomy is the surgical removal of the breasts to prevent breast cancer in women who are at high risk of developing the disease

Risk factors include:

- First onset of menstrual cycle at an early age or late menopause.

- Women who had no children or first child later in life or women who did not nurse.

- Women who used hormone replacement therapy (HRT).

- Women who consume high-fat diets and lead sedentary lifestyles.

- Women with a family history of breast cancer and who carry mutated tumor suppressor genes.

Breast Self-Examination (BSE) procedures should be performed after age 20 during the menstrual cycle or a day after. Proper techniques can be found at Memorial Sloan-Kettering Cancer Center at http://www.mskcc.org.

Mammography

The best tool for early detection of breast cancer is routine mammography. The American Cancer Society recommends that mammography begin at age 40. Women with a family history of breast cancer should begin at age 35 or younger. For women over 65, mammography screening frequency is a matter of individual recommendations from the physician.

Prostate Cancer

The prostate gland is located near the base of the penis and surrounds the bladder and urethra. This walnut-sized gland secretes fluids responsible for sperm mortality.

Second to skin cancer, prostate cancer is the most common cancer in men and is the second leading cause of cancer deaths in men. About 1 in 6 men will be diagnosed with prostate cancer in their lifetime. According to the American Cancer Society, an estimated 180,890 prostate cancer diagnoses will be made in 2016, and an estimated 26,120 men will die from prostate cancer. Prostate cancer cases are higher among Black men than their White counterparts.

Early detection and diagnosis have resulted in about 4% decline since 2012.

Risk factors for prostate cancer are not clear but include:

- Age is the most predictable risk factor. Majority of diagnosed cases are in men 65 years old and older.

- Being an African-American man

- Family history

- Dietary fat and red meat

- Genetic mutation

Pancreatic Cancer

Pancreatic cancer, also referred to as exocrine cancer (95% exocrine pancreas which produces enzymes responsible for digestion) affects the tissue surrounding the pancreas. In 2016, an estimated 53,070 new cases will be diagnosed in the United States and 41,7800 deaths in both men and women combined will occur, according to the National Cancer Institute.

Risk factors include:

- Age

- Male gender

- Diabetes

- Being African-American

- Family history

- Smoking

- Chronic pancreatitis

Symptoms include:

- Nausea and vomiting

- Weight loss

- Weakness

- Yellowing of the eyes and skin and dark urine caused by jaundice

- Pain in the upper abdomen or back

Colon and Rectal Cancer

According to the American Cancer Society, an estimated 95,270 colon and 39,220 rectal cancer cases will be diagnosed in 2016. Estimated deaths from colorectal cancer were 49,190. Deaths from colorectal cancer have have declined since 2012. Two types of tumors, carcinoma and lymphoma, have been linked to colorectal cancer. With early detection, relative survivability rate from this cancer is as high as 90 percent.

Risk factors include:

- Genetic predisposition

- High-fat diets and red meat

Prevention includes:

- Removal of polyps

- Regular exercise

- Calcium intake

- Folic acid supplement

- Consistent low-dose aspirin (81 mg)

- Regular checkups—rectal exam after age 40 and stool blood test after age 50

Cervical Cancer

Four decades ago, cervical cancer was the leading cause of death for women in the United States. Although intervention strategies through Pap tests have significantly lowered the mortality rates, the Human Papilloma Virus remains the most significant risk factor for cervical cancer. Epidemiological data from all over the world have shown the presence of HPV in 95% of cervical cancer occurrences. Each year, there are about 13,000 diagnosed cervical cancer cases for American women. According to the National Cancer Institute, there will be 12,990 new cases and 4,120 deaths reported in 2016. The National Cervical Cancer Public Education Campaign recommends that every sexually active woman be screened for cervical cancer. Exceptions apply only to those women who have had a total hysterectomy for reasons other than to treat cancer. The Gardasil vaccine by Merck has been proven to be effective in preventing HPVs 16 and 18 strains that cause cervical cancer.

Risk factors include:

- Early age of first intercourse

- Large number of sexual partners

- History of infertility

- Clinical presence of HPV

- Cigarette smoking

- Socioecomomic factors

Skin Cancer

Many forms of skin cancer will permanently change a person's appearance. Skin cancer is the most common type of all cancers. The sun is responsible for over one million cases of non-melanoma skin cancer found in the United States each year. According to the American Cancer Society, an esitmated 76,380 basal skin cancer cases will be diagnosed in 2016, with 10,130 deaths from melanoma and 3,520 from other types of skin cancer.

Risk factors include:

- Severe sunburn during childhood

- Fair complexion

- Family history

- Occupational exposure to coal, tar, pitch, creosote, arsenic compounds, or radium

Prevention includes:

- Use of sunscreen with a sun protection factor (SPF) of 15 or greater

- Avoiding sun exposure between 11:00 A.M. and 2:00 P.M.

Skin cancer can be detected early, and both doctor and patient play a role in finding the cancer. It is important for people to know what to look for during self-examination. Moles often start as normal-looking but change in size or color and acquire abnormal characteristics. A simple ABCD rule outlines the warning signs of melanoma:

- Asymmetry—one half of the mole does not match the other half

- Border irregularity—edges are uneven, notched or scalloped

- Color—pigmentation is not uniform. Melanoma may vary in color from tan to deeper brown, reddish-black, black, or deep bluish-black

- Diameter—the diameter is greater than 6 millimeters (about the size of a pea)

Asymmetry   Border irregularity

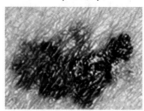   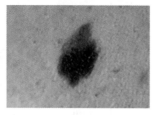

Color   Diameter: ¼ inch or 6 mm

The Seven Warning Signs of Cancer

The American Cancer Society has developed a list of seven early warning signs for cancer. The first letter in each word spells out the word CAUTION:

C hange in bowel or bladder habits

A sore that does not heal

U nusual bleeding or discharge

T hickening of lump in breast or elsewhere

I ndigestion or difficulty swallowing

O bvious change in a mole or wart

N agging cough or hoarseness

By paying close attention to these warning signs, the earlier cancer can be diagnosed, the better chance for treatment.

Cancer Treatment

Treatments for cancer include chemotherapy, radiation, surgery, drug therapy, and acupuncture. Treatment options will depend on the patient's choice and cancer stages.

Guidelines for Preventing Cancer

1. Avoid tobacco use in all forms. Smoking is correlated to 85% of lung cancer cases.

2. Eat a low-fat, high-fiber diet. Numerous studies have found links between diet and cancer. High risk diets are those that are high in calories and fat, and low in fiber.

3. Eat more cruciferous vegetables (cabbage, cauliflower, etc.). These help to reduce the risk of cancers such as colon cancer.

4. Avoid smoked or charcoal carcinogens.

5. Use alcohol in moderation. Heavy drinkers have increased oral and esophageal cancers.

6. Avoid being overweight. Excess body weight and fat produces hormones that may promote cancerous growth.

7. Engage in aerobic exercise 4 times a week for at least 30 minutes.

8. Avoid sexually transmitted infections (STIs)—STI viruses have been linked to cancers of the cervix and penis.

9. Reduce sunlight exposure.

   - Avoid sunlamps.

   - Use sun block even when clouds are present.

   - Reapply sun block after swimming.

10. Do regular self-exams for early detection.

    - Men—testicular cancer

    - Women—breast cancer

11. Get a yearly checkup by a health care provider.

Summary Questions

1. Cancer is a destructive disease. Describe its impact on the body.

2. What prevention methods are available to reduce your risk for contracting skin cancer?

3. Why is lung cancer the leading cause of cancer deaths?

4. What are the warning signs of cancer?

5. Explain how lifestyle changes can reduce your cancer risk.

References

Encyclopedia of Epidemiology, 2008, ISBN 1412928168

Green Health (2011): An A-to-Z Guide, ISBN 1412974593

Hahn, D.B.; Payne, W.A.; & Lucas, E.B. (2011). *Focus on Health*, 10th. Ed. New York, NY: McGraw-Hill.

Krege, S. (2011). *What is new in 2011 regarding testicular cancer?* Der Urologe. Ausg. A, 501, pp. 187–19.

Siegal, R.; Naishadham, M.; & Ahmedin, J. (2012). *Cancer Statics 2012. A Cancer Journal for Clinicians*, 62: 1: doi.10.3322/caac.20138.

Villers, A.; Haffner, J.; & Bouye, S. (2008). What is prostate cancer? *Bulletin De L Academie Nationale Medicine*, 192, Issue 5, pp. 1003–1011.

Web Sites

http://www.aicr.org
American Institute for Cancer Research

http://www.nci.nih.gov
National Cancer Institute

http://www.cdc.gov
The Centers for Disease Control and Prevention

http://www.diseaseriskindex.harvard.edu/update/
Harvard Center for Cancer Prevention

http://www.cancer.org
American Cancer Society

http://www.lungusa.org
American Lung Association

http://www.cancer.gov
National Cancer Institute

chapter 12

Special Topics
Sexually Transmitted Infections

by Christopher S. Ousley, M. Ed.

The continual rise of Sexually Transmitted Infections (STIs) is the result of several factors. One of these factors is a rise in sexual activity with many individuals having multiple partners. Another factor is that the use of spermicides and condoms has decreased as the use of birth control pills has increased. Many STIs do not produce obvious symptoms, so people are often unaware that they have an STI. Feelings of guilt, embarrassment, and denial may prevent people from seeking adequate treatment. In the next section, six of the most well-known STIs will be examined.

Chlamydia

In the 1980s, chlamydia was recognized as a widespread STI. Chlamydia is caused by bacterial infection. It invades the cells it attacks, and multiplies within them like a virus. It is among the most prevalent and most damaging of STIs. The Center for Disease Control (CDC) estimates 3 million infections per year in the United States.

Transmission is primarily through sexual contact. It may be spread by fingers from one body site to another, such as genitals to eyes. Genital chlamydia infection in females can include infections of lower reproductive tract (urethritis or cervicitis) and infections of upper reproductive tract (pelvic inflammatory disease). Pelvic inflammatory disease (PID) is an infection of the lining of the uterus, fallopian tubes, and possibly the ovaries and adjacent abdominal structures. Chlamydia may account for as many as a half of a million annual U.S. cases of PID.

Around 70% of infected people have no early symptoms. Symptoms occur 1 to 3 weeks after exposure. Most women with lower reproductive tract chlamydia infections have few or no symptoms. In men, chlamydia is estimated to be the cause of half of the cases of epididymitis and nongonococcal urethritis.

12

Chapter
Twelve

Gonorrhea (Clap)

There are 650,000 reported cases each year and an estimated 1 million overall including unreported cases in the United States. Gonorrhea is caused by a bacterial infection. It grows in mucous membranes. The bacteria survive in warm mucous membranes of the genitals, anus, and throat. It is transmitted by sexual contact, vaginal intercourse, oral sex, and anal sex.

Early symptoms in the male appear within 1 to 5 days after contact. However, symptoms may show up as late as 2 weeks later, or, in a small percentage of cases, not at all. Early symptoms sometimes clear up on their own without treatment; however, the bacteria often moves on to other organs such as the prostate, bladder, kidneys, and testicles. It may move down the vas deferens, inflaming the epididymis and causing scar tissue, which can block the flow of sperm. If the infection is untreated, it can cause sterility in both females and males.

As many as 80% of females have no early symptoms and are unaware of the infection. The primary site of infection is the cervix, which becomes inflamed without observable symptoms. A green or yellowish discharge usually results, and may go undetected. There is an increased risk of PID as the bacteria moves upward.

Syphilis

There are 20,000 reported cases each year in the U.S. Some STI specialists speculate that as many as nine cases go unreported for each one recorded. Syphilis is an STI caused by thin, corkscrew-like bacterium (*treponema pallidum*—spirochete). It is transmitted from open lesions to mucous membranes or skin abrasions of partners through penile–vaginal, oral–genital, or genital–anal contact. There are four classes of syphilis: primary, secondary, latent, and tertiary.

1. Primary
   Approximately 10 to 90 days (average 21 days) after exposure, a chancre appears at site where spirochete enters the body. In women, the sore appears on the inner wall of the vagina, cervix, or on the labia. In men, it most often appears on the glans of penis, penile shaft, or scrotum. It often goes undiscovered on internal structures. The chancre generally heals without treatment in 4 to 6 weeks.

2. Secondary
   A skin rash appears usually on the palms of hands and the soles of feet. Raised bumps develop that have a rubbery, hard consistency that typically does not hurt or itch. Other symptoms are fever, swollen lymph glands, fatigue, weight loss, and sores. Symptoms subside within a few weeks and enter the next stage.

3. Latent
   This stage can last for several years. More than half of untreated syphilis victims remain in the latent stage for the rest of their lives. There may be no observable symptoms. Organisms may continue to multiply, preparing for the final stage.

4. Tertiary
   The final stage can be severe, resulting in death. Bacteria multiply and attack various organs and tissues. This stage can occur anywhere from 3 to 40 years after infection and may cause heart failure, blindness, ruptured blood vessels, paralysis, liver damage, and severe mental disturbances.

Herpes

Approximately 100 million Americans have oral herpes and 50 million have genital herpes. Herpes is caused by herpes simplex virus (HSV). A virus is an organism that invades, reproduces, and lives within a cell. The most common are HSV–1 (usually sores appear on/around mouth and lips) and HSV–2 (usually sores appear on/around genital areas). About 20% of genital herpes is linked to HSV–1. There are an estimated 1 million new cases of genital herpes each year. Transmission of genital herpes occurs primarily by penile–vaginal, oral–genital, or genital–anal contact. Transmission of oral herpes occurs from kissing.

When sores are present, the person is highly contagious. The virus can be spread from one part of body to another by touching a sore and then scratching elsewhere, a process known as autinoculation. Herpes in the eyes, keratitis, can damage the cornea. Not all individuals experience recognizable symptoms. In women, symptoms occur on the labia, inner walls of the vagina, and the cervix. In men, symptoms occur on the glans or the shaft of the penis. Red bumps develop into tiny, painful blisters filled with a clear fluid containing virus particles. The body attacks the virus with white blood cells, causing blisters to become filled with pus. Blisters rupture to form wet, painful, open sores surrounded by a red ring. Open sores form a crust and then begin to heal, which may take up to two weeks. Avoid contact for 10 days after the sores have healed. Sores on the cervix take much longer to heal. Infection may take up to 4 weeks to heal.

Many individuals have periodic flare-ups. In cases of HSV–2, 7% to 30% of patients have at least one recurrence. Studies show that the more extensive the primary attack, the greater the chance of recurrence. Of those who experience recurrence, as many as 75% experience prodromal symptoms (itching, burning, throbbing, tingling at sites, sometimes pain in legs, thighs, groin, or buttocks) which give advance warning of eruption. An individual's infectiousness increases during this stage. Factors that may trigger reactivation of herpes include emotional stress which can weaken the immune system, sunburn, cold, poor nutrition, and being over-tired or exhausted.

HPV (Human Papillomavirus) or Genital Warts

In 1992, HPV became the most common viral STI in the U.S. The incidence is rapidly increasing in both sexes with 35 million reported cases. 1–5 million new cases happen each year. There are about 100 strains of HPV, of which 7 cause outgrowth of warts. HPV is transmitted by skin-to-skin contact, where one individuals infects the other by transmitting the virus. The incubation period ranges from 3 weeks to 3 months. In many cases, the warts are not largely visible and may go undetected in the early stages. In moist areas, they are pink/red and soft with a cauliflower-like appearance. In dry areas, they are generally hard and yellow-gray. Some people carry the virus without developing any symptoms. There is a strong association between HPV and cancers of the cervix, vagina, vulva, penis, and anus.

A vaccine named Gardasil was approved in 2006 to prevent infection of the four most common types of HPV strains. The vaccine is designed to prevent cervical cancer linked to HPV.

STD	SYMPTOMS	DIAGNOSIS	TREATMENT
Chlamydia	**Females:** • Mild irritation • Itching of genital tissues • Burning during urination • Slight discharge *PID symptoms* • Disrupted menstrual periods • Pain in the lower abdomen • Elevated temperature • Nausea • Vomiting • Ectopic pregnancy may also occur **Males:** • Burning sensation during urination and discharge of pus • Sensation of heaviness in the affected testicle • Inflammation of scrotal skin • Formation of small area of hard painful swelling of the testicle	• Obtain urethral or cervical discharge, grow a culture and examine the culture. • A urine test that detects bacterial DNA in the urine.	• Treated and cured with a week of antibiotic drugs such as erythromycin and doxycycline. • Penicillin is not effective.
Gonorrhea (Clap)	• Foul-smelling yellowish-green, cloudy discharge from the penis • Burning sensations during urination	• A smear is made of the discharge and examined microscopically. • A culture is grown and then examined. • An application of an enzyme-sensitive immunoassay can detect gonorrhea.	• Penicillin used to be the cure-all; however, there are now penicillin-resistant strains, so patients may use ceftriaxone, azithromycin, and doxycycline.

STD	SYMPTOMS	DIAGNOSIS	TREATMENT
Herpes	• Small painful, red bumps which usually appear between 2 and 12 days after sexual contact.	• Direct observation. • Cultures of virus grown in lab.	• Antiviral drugs, such as acyclovir, to reduce discomfort and speed healing during the initial outbreak. • Use of valacylclovir has been shown to both suppress and reduce duration or outbreaks.
Syphilis	**Primary** • Painless sore ("chancre")—10 to 90 days after exposure, at site where spirochete enters the body. • 95% of chancres are on the genitals; others occur in the mouth, lips, tongue, rectum or anus. . **Secondary** • Skin rash on hands and feet. • Raised bumps with rubbery, hard consistency (typically, does not hurt or itch). • Fever, swollen lymph glands, fatigue, weight loss and sores. **Latent** • May be no observable symptoms. **Tertiary** • Severe, may result in death.	• Blood tests. • Microscopic examination of fluid from chancre.	• Primary and secondary syphilis treated with a single intramuscular injection of penicillin. If the patient is allergic, then tetracycline erythromycin can be prescribed. Latent and tertiary syphilis requires larger doses of antibiotics over a period of several weeks.
HPV (Human Papilloma virus) or Genital Warts	**Females:** • Warts appear at the bottom part of vaginal opening, perineum, labia, inner walls of vagina and cervix. **Males:** • Warts commonly occur on glans, foreskin and shaft of penis.	• Observation. • Tissue biopsy.	• Remove by laser. • Treat with acid. • Topical applications (podophyllin). • Freeze with liquid nitrogen. • Surgical removal. • The virus remains in the body and warts can often reappear.

HIV: Human Immunodeficiency Virus

In the U.S., there are up to 1 million people with HIV and 40,000 new cases of HIV each year. Worldwide, there are 33 million people infected with HIV, with over 3 million new infections each year. HIV causes AIDS. It took 8 years to record the first 100,000 AIDS cases, and just 2 years for the next 100,000 cases.

The most common fluids involved in the transmission of HIV are blood, semen, and vaginal secretions. The virus can be transmitted in the womb and through breast milk. HIV is found in saliva, tears, urine, and feces, but the possibility of transmission from these fluids has been shown to be unlikely.

Routes of HIV Infection

1. Vaginal or anal intercourse

2. Oral–genital sex

3. Contact with infected semen or vaginal fluids

4. Infected organ transplant and infected blood

5. Use of contaminated needles

6. Transfer from mother to infant during childbirth

HIV's Impact upon the Immune System

HIV is a retrovirus which consists of a protein shell surrounding the genetic material RNA. HIV attaches to T-lymphocytes known as CD4s, a type of white blood cell, and injects its RNA into the CD4 cell. RNA is then converted into DNA by an enzyme called reverse transcriptase. The HIV DNA hijacks the CD4's DNA, causing the cell to become a viral factory. Numerous viral particles are produced, and then they break through the CD4 membrane, causing cellular death, and go on to invade other CD4 cells. Over time, this action suppresses the immune system, leaving the individual vulnerable to other infectious agents.

HIV Infection Stages

There are four stages of HIV infection. The duration of these stages varies according to the person's health.

1. Primary HIV disease occurs soon after being infected with HIV. Some people experience a fever, swollen glands, and fatigue. They may think they have the flu. As the immune system charges into action, these symptoms usually subside within a couple of weeks.

2. Chronic asymptomatic disease is a decline in the immune cells with no specific disease symptoms.

3. Chronic symptomatic disease is a major depletion of immune cells, leaving the body vulnerable to opportunistic infections. One common infection is a yeast infection of the mouth called thrush. Other symptoms during this stage are fevers, diarrhea, night sweats, and weight loss.

4. AIDS: Diagnosis is made after one or more of 26 diseases has appeared. An example is pnuemocystis carinii which is pneumonia caused by a proliferation of a fungus due to a suppressed immune system.

HIV Testing

When someone becomes infected with HIV, the body begins to produce antibodies in an attempt to destroy the virus. Antibodies to the virus are what HIV tests are trying to detect. Generally, antibodies show up anywhere from 6 weeks to 6 months after infection. Thus, a person may be advised to get another test 6 months later after their last suspected infection incident. The local health department can administer an HIV test.

Prevention of STIs

Abstinence is the most effective way to avoid sexually transmitted infections. Abstinence is defined differently according to different groups. Some would state that abstinence can be defined as not engaging in vaginal intercourse. Thus, those only engaging in oral–genital sex would be defined as abstinent according to the previous definition.

Here, abstinence will be defined as not engaging in any type of sexual contact such as penile–vaginal, penile–anal, oral–genital, mutual masturbation, or cross-contact of penile/vaginal fluids.

People choose abstinence for a variety of reasons. Some of these include fear of pregnancy and STIs, health issues, moral/religious purposes, and because they have no current relationship. For those who do not choose abstinence, be clear about your boundaries. Make sure your partner knows what sexual activities that you will participate in and the ones that you will not. Research various methods of contraception, in order to avoid pregnancy, to choose the one that will work best for your lifestyle and medical history. In conclusion, the only method of contraception that works 100% of the time in the prevention of STIs is abstinence.

Summary Questions

1. What % of people do not have early symptoms of chlamydia?

2. List two symptoms of gonorrhea.

3. List and explain the 4 stages of a syphilis infection.

4. Under the section on herpes, explain prodromal symptoms.

5. How many strains of HPV cause genital warts?

6. Explain the four stages of an HIV infection.

7. Where can one go to get tested for HIV?

References

Kelly, G.F. (2011). *Sexuality Today: The Human Perspective* (10th ed.) New York, NY: McGraw-Hill.

Rosenthal, M.S. (2012). *Human Sexuality: From Cells to Society* (1st ed.) Belmont, CA: Wadsworth, Cengage Learning.

Web Sites

http://www.ashastd.org
American Social Health Association

http://www.cdc.gov/nchhstp/
CDC Center for STD Prevention

http://www.cdcnpin.org/
Prevention Information Network

AIDS: Acquired Immunodeficiency Syndrome
Hotline: 800-342-AIDS (2437)

Clearinghouse: http://www.cdc.gov